HINDU DHARMA

M.K. GANDHI

AF657903

RUSTAM PRAKASHAN

All rights reserved. No part of this publication may be reproduced, stored in a retrieval system, or transmitted, in any form, or by any means, electronic, mechanical, photocopying, recording or otherwise, without the prior permission of the publishers.

ISBN: 978-93-59918-21-1
eISBN: 978-81-96549-36-7

©Publishers

Publisher: **Rustam Prakashan**
Address: 5th Floor, Flat No. E-502,
Dwarkadham Apartment, Block-E Plot No-13
Sec-23, Mahajan Shree CGHS Ltd,
New Delhi, South West, 110077
Phone: 011-40395855
WhatsApp: +91 9319228272
E-mail: rustamprakashan@gmail.com
Edition: 2023

Hindu Dharma
Author: M.K. Gandhi

PUBLISHER'S NOTE

Mohandas Karamchand Gandhi (1869-1948), popularly known as Mahatma Gandhi, is a political and moral leader from India. He is known for mobilizing the masses in his non-violent resistance against the British rule in India. His *satyagraha* (protest of truth) against the colonial rule played an eminent role in India's independence, because of which, he is regarded as the 'Father of the Nation'.

Gandhi's ideologies of *Ahimsa* (non-violence) and Truth have been adopted by thousands around the world and have proved immensely popular. These ideologies were borrowed by Gandhi from his interpretations of the Hindu Scriptures and Hindu philosophy, particularly that of the 'Gita'. Throughout his lifetime, Gandhi engaged himself with the discourse of Hindu philosophy which is reflected in his writings and speeches. He has in fact vividly discussed the matters of philosophy in his speeches and writings, particularly published in *Young India*, to provide ways for social and political progress of the society. On the 150th anniversary of Mahatma Gandhi, it is an immense pleasure for us at **Pharos Books**, to publish the rich legacy that he has left behind. We hope and wish that his works will inspire the youth to do better and be better.

Contents

CHAPTER-1

Why I am a Hindu

An American friend who subscribes herself as a lifelong friend of India writes:

> As Hinduism is one of the prominent religions of the East, and as you have made a study of Christianity and Hinduism, and on the basis of that study have announced that you are a Hindu, I beg leave to ask of you if you will do me the favour to give me your reasons for that choice. Hindus and Christians alike realise that man's chief need is to know God and to worship Him in spirit and in truth. Believing that Christ was a revelation of God, Christians of America have sent to India thousands of their sons and daughters to tell the people of India about Christ. Will you in return kindly give us your interpretation of Hinduism and make a comparison of Hinduism with the teachings of Christ? I will be deeply grateful for this favour.

I have ventured at several missionary meetings to tell English and American could have refrained from 'telling' India about Christ and had merely lived the life enjoined upon them by the Sermon on the Mount, India instead of suspecting them would have appreciated their living in the midst of her children and directly profited by their presence. Holding this view, I can 'tell' American friends nothing about Hinduism by way of 'return'. I do not believe in people telling others of their faith, especially with a view to conversion. Faith does not admit to telling. It has to be lived and then it becomes self-propagating.

Nor do I consider myself fit to interpret Hinduism except through my own life. And if I may not interpret-Hinduism through my written word, I may not compare it with Christianity. The only thing it is possible for me therefore to do is to say, as briefly as I can, why I am a Hindu.

Believing as I do in the influence of heredity, being born in a Hindu family, I have remained a Hindu. I should reject it, if I found it inconsistent with my moral sense or my spiritual growth. On examination, I have found it to be the most tolerant of all religions known to me. Its freedom from dogma makes a forcible appeal to me inasmuch as it gives the votary the largest scope for self-expression. Not being an exclusive religion, it enables the followers of that faith not merely to respect all the other religions, but it also enables them to admire and assimilate whatever may be good in the other faiths. Non-violence is common to all religions, but it has found the highest expression and application in Hinduism. (I do not regard Jainism or Buddhism as separate from Hinduism). Hinduism believes in the oneness not of merely all human life but in the oneness of till that lives. Its worship of the cow is, in my opinion, its unique contribution to the evolution of humanitarianism. Itis a practical application of the belief in the oneness and, therefore, sacredness of all life. The great belief in transmigration is a direct consequence of that belief. Finally, the discovery of the law of *varnashrama* is a magnificent result of the ceaseless search for truth. I must not burden this article with definitions of the essentials sketched here, except to say that the present ideas of cow-worship and *varnashrama* appeared in the previous numbers of *Young India*. I hope to have to say more on *varnashrama* in the near future. In this all-too-brief a sketch I have mentioned what occurs to me to be the outstanding features of Hinduism that keep me in its fold.

CHAPTER-2

Aspects of Hinduism

In dealing with the problem of untouchability during the Madras tour, I have asserted my claim to being a *sanatani* Hindu with greater emphasis than hitherto, and yet there are things which are commonly done in the name of Hinduism, which I disregard. I have no desire to be called a *sanatani* Hindu or any other if I am not such. And I have certainly no desire to steal in a reform or an abuse under cover of a great faith.

It is, therefore, necessary for me once and for all distinctly to give my meaning oi *sanatana Windvism*. The word *sanatana* I use in its natural sense.

I call myself a *sanatani* Hindu, because,

1. I believe in the Vedas, the Upanishads, the Puranas and all that goes by the name of Hindu scriptures, and therefore in *avatars and* rebirth,
2. I believe in the *varnashrama* dharma in a sense in my opinion strictly Vedic, but not in its present popular and crude sense,
3. I believe in the protection of the cow in its much larger sense than the popular, and
4. I do not disbelieve in idol-worship.'

The reader will note that I have purposely refrained from using the word divine origin in reference to the Vedas or any other scriptures. For, I do not believe in the exclusive divinity of the Vedas. I believe the Bible, the Koran, and the Zend-Avesta to be as much divinely inspired as the Vedas. My belief in the Hindu scriptures does not require me to accept every word and every verse as divinely inspired. Nor do I claim to have any first-hand knowledge of these wonderful books. But I do claim to know and feel the truths of the essential teaching of the scriptures. I decline to be bound by any interpretation, however, learned it may be, if it is repugnant to reason or moral sense. I do most emphatically repudiate the claim (if they advance any such) of the present Shankaracharyas and *shastris* to give a correct interpretation of the Hindu scriptures. On the contrary, I believe that our present knowledge of these books is in a most chaotic state. I believe implicitly in the Hindu aphorism, that no one truly knows the Shastras who has not attained perfection in innocence *(ahimsa)*, truth *(satya)* and self- control *(brahmacharya)*, and who has not renounced all acquisition or possession of wealth. I believe in the institution of *gurus*, but in this age, millions must go without a *guru*, because it is a rare thing to find a combination of perfect purity and perfect learning. But one need not despair of ever knowing the truth of one's religion, because the fundamentals of Hinduism as of every great religion are unchangeable, and easily understood. Every Hindu believes in God and his oneness, in rebirth and salvation. But that which distinguishes Hinduism from every other religion is its cow-protection, more than its *varnashrama*.

Varnashrama is, in my opinion, inherent in human nature, and Hinduism have simply reduced it to a science. It does attach to birth. A man cannot change his *varna* by choice. Not to abide by one's *varna* is to disregard the law of heredity. The division, however, into innumerable castes is an unwarranted liberty taken with the doctrine. The four divisions are all-sufficing.

I do not believe that inter-dining or even intermarriage necessarily deprives a man of his status that his birth has given him. The four divisions define a man's calling, they do not restrict or regulate social intercourse. The divisions define duties, they confer no privileges. It is, I hold, against the genius of Hinduism to arrogate to oneself a higher status or assign to another a lower. All are born to serve God's creation, a Brahmin with his knowledge, a Kshatriya with his power of protection, a Vaisya with his commercial ability and a Sudra with his bodily labour. This, however, does not mean that a Brahmin, for instance, is absolved from bodily labour, or the duty of protecting himself and others. His birth makes a Brahmin predominantly a man of knowledge, the fittest by heredity and training to impart it to others. There is nothing, again, to prevent the Sudra from acquiring all the knowledge he wishes. Only, he will best serve with his body and need not envy others their special qualities for service. But a Brahmin who claims superiority by right of knowledge falls, and has no knowledge. And so with the others who pride themselves upon their special qualities. *Varnashrama* is self-restraint and conservation and economy of energy.

Though therefore *varnashrama* is not affected by inter-dining or

inter-marriage, Hinduism does most emphatically discourage inter-dining and inter-marriage between divisions. Hinduism reached the highest limit of self-restraint. It is undoubtedly a religion of renunciation of the flesh so that the spirit may be set free. It is no part of a Hindu's duty to dine with his son. And by restricting his choice of a bride to a particular group, he exercises rare self-restraint. Hinduism does not regard a married state as by any more essential for salvation. Marriage is a 'fall' even as birth is a 'fall'. Salvation is freedom from birth and hence death also. Prohibition against inter-marriage and inter-dining is essential for a rapid evolution of the soul. But this self-denial is no test of *varna*. A Brahmin may remain a Brahmin, though he may dine with his Sudra brother, if he has not left off his duty of service by knowledge. It follows from what I have said above, that restraint in matters of marriage and dining is not based upon notions of superiority. A Hindu who refuses to dine with another from a sense of superiority misrepresents his *dharma*.

Unfortunately, today Hinduism seems to consist merely in eating and not-eating. Once I horrified a pious Hindu by taking toast at a Mussulman's house. I saw, that he was pained to see me pouring milk into a cup handed by a Mussulman friend, but his anguish knew no bounds when he saw me taking toast at the Mussulman's hands. Hinduism is in danger of losing its substance if it resolves itself into a matter of elaborate rules as to what and with whom to eat. Abstemiousness from intoxicating drinks and drugs, and from all kinds of foods, especially meat, is undoubtedly a great aid to the evolution of the spirit, but it is by no means an end in itself. Many a man eating meat with everybody, but living in the fear of God, is nearer his freedom than a man religiously abstaining from meat and many other things, but blaspheming God in every one of his acts.

The central fact of Hinduism however is cow-protection. Cow- protection to me is one of the most wonderful phenomena in human evolution. It takes the human being beyond his species. The cow is enjoined to realize his identity with all that lives. Why the cow was selected for apotheosis is obvious to me. The cow was in India the best companion.

She was the giver of plenty. Not only did she give milk, but she also made agriculture possible. The cow is a poem of pity. One reads pity in the gentle animal. She is the mother to millions of Indian mankind. Protection of the cow means protection of the whole dumb creation of God. The ancient seer, whoever he was, began with the *cow*. The appeal of the lower order of creation is all the more forcible because it is speechless. Cow-protection is the gift of Hinduism to the world. And Hinduism will live so long as there are Hindus to protect the cow.

The way to protect is to die for her. It is a denial of Hinduism and *ahimsa* to kill a human being to protect a cow. Hindus are enjoined to protect the cow by their *tapasya*, by self-purification, by self-sacrifice. The present day cow-protection has degenerated into a perpetual feud With the Mussulmans, whereas cow-protection means conquering Mussulmans by our love. A Mussulman friend sent me some time ago a book detailing the inhumanities practiced by us on the cow put her progeny. How we bleed her to take the last drop of milk from her, how we starve her to emaciation, how we ill-treat the calves, how we deprive them of their portion of milk, how cruelly we treat the oxen, how we castrate them, how we beat them, how we deprive them. If they had speech, they would bear witness to our crimes against them which would stagger the world. By every act of cruelty to our cattle, we disown God and Hinduism. I do not know that the condition of the cattle in any other part of the world is as bad as in unhappy India. We may not blame the Englishman for this. We may plead poverty in our defence. Criminal negligence is the only cause of the condition of our cattle. Our *pinjrapoles*, though they are an answer to our instinct of mercy, are a clumsy demonstration of its execution. Instead of being model dairy farms and great profitable national institutions, they are merely depots for receiving decrepit cattle.

Hindus will be judged not by their *tilaks*, not by the correct chanting of *mantras*, not by their pilgrimages, not by their most punctilious observance of caste rules but by their ability to protect the cow. Whilst professing the religion of cow-protection, we have enslaved the cow and her progeny, and have become slaves ourselves.

It will now be understood why I consider myself a *sanatani* Hindu. I yield to none in my regard for the cow. I have made the Khilafat cause my own, because I see that through its preservation full protection can be secured for the cow. I do not ask my Mussulman friends to save the cow in consideration of my service. My prayer ascends daily to God Almighty, that my service of a cause I hold to be just may appear so pleasing to Him, that He may change the hearts of the Mussulmans, and fill them with pity for their Hindu neighbours and make them save the animal the latter hold dear as life itself.

I can no more describe my feeling for Hinduism than for my own wife. She moves me as no other woman in the world can. Not that she has no-fault. I dare say she has many more than I see myself. But the feeling of an indissoluble bond is there. Even so I feel for and about Hinduism with all its faults and limitations. Nothing elates me so much as the music of the 'Gita' or the 'Ramayana' by Tulsidas, the only two books in Hinduism I may be said to know. When I fancied I was taking my last breath, the 'Gita' was my solace. I know the vice that is going on today in all the great Hindu shrines, but I love them in spite of their unspeakable failings. There is an interest which I take in them and which I take in no other. I am a reformer through and through. But my zeal never takes me to the rejection of any of the essential things of Hinduism. I have said I do not disbelieve in idol-worship. An idol does not excite any feeling of veneration in me. But I think that idol-worship is part of human nature. We hanker after symbolism. Why should one be more composed in a church than elsewhere? Images are an aid to worship. No Hindu considers an image to be God. I do not consider idol-worship a sin.

It is clear from the foregoing, that Hinduism is not exclusive religion. In it, there is room for the worship of all the prophets of the world. It is not a missionary religion in the ordinary sense of the term. It has doubt absorbed many tribes in its fold, but this absorption has been of an evolutionary imperceptible character. Hinduism tells everyone to worship God according to his own faith or *dharma*, and so it lives at peace with all the religions.

That being my conception of Hinduism, I have never been able to reconcile myself to untouchability. I have always regarded it as an excrescence. It is true that it has been handed down to us from generations, but so are many evil practices even to this day. I ashamed to think that dedication of girls to virtual prostitution was a part of Hinduism. Yet it is practised by Hindus in many parts of India. I consider it positively irreligious to sacrifice goats to Kali and do not consider it a part of Hinduism. Hinduism is a growth of ages. The very name, Hinduism, was given to the religion of the people of Hindustan by foreigners. There was no doubt at one time sacrifice of animals offered in the name of religion. But it is not religion, much less is it Hindu religion. And so also it seems to me, that when cow-protection became an article of faith with our ancestors, those who persisted in eating beef were excommunicated. The civil strife must have been fierce. Social boycott was applied not only to the recalcitrant, but their sins were visited upon their children also. The practice which had probably its origin in good intentions hardened into usage, and even verses crept in our sacred books giving the practice a permanence wholly undeserved and still less justified. Whether my theory is correct or not, untouchability is repugnant to reason and to the instinct of mercy, pity or love. A religion that establishes the worship of the cow cannot possibly countenance or warrant a cruel and inhuman boycott of human beings. And I should be content to be torn to pieces rather than disown the suppressed classes. Hindus will certainly never deserve freedom, nor get it if they allow their noble religion to be disgraced by the retention of the taint of untouchability. And as I love Hinduism dearer than life itself, the taint has become for me an intolerable burden. Let us not deny God by denying to a fifth of our race the right of association on an equal footing.

CHAPTER-3

Some Problems

A dear friend sends me a letter gently criticizing the manner of my defence of Maulana Mahomed Ali's now famous speech regarding his comparison of creeds. The friend says that I have not been fair to Hinduism in that I have said a Hindu will fare no better than the Maulana. He quarrels with my illustration about marriage and then goes on to show the beauties of Hinduism. Another friend, too, has made a similar remonstrance and added that many others share his opinion.

These friends have, in my opinion, mixed up the question of propriety of comparing creeds with that of the allocation of their respective merits. Indeed, in arguing that Hinduism is not like Islam and that the Hindu could not think like the Maulana, the friends themselves have subscribed to the Maulana's argument that it is not only perfectly correct, but it is the logical outcome of one's preferring a particular belief to every other, that for oneself that particular belief, though held by a bad man, is superior to that of another howsoever saintly. I adhere to the marriage illustration chosen by me, though I now see that it would have been better for me to have avoided it. It is not a conclusive illustration. There are, I admit with my critics, many reasons for confining the choice of a husband to a particular class. But I do claim that the predominant reason for excluding the best man if he happens to belong, as he often does, to another class or caste is his creed. A Brahmin parent chooses a Brahmin as a husband for his daughter because he prefers the general body of opinion, which may be called, creed, held by his clan. Underlying the preference is no doubt the belief that acceptance of a creed ultimately involves practice in accordance with it. A narrow creed, if it is honestly believed, has necessarily a limited field for practice. A creed, for instance, that makes it obligatory to offer human sacrifice will never free the believer from the taint of religious murder unless he gives up the creed. Thus it is that we find people, otherwise most moral, disappointing us when they fall short of the highest because of their narrow creed. Many sincere and otherwise noble-minded Hindus consider untouchability as a part of the Hindu creed and would, therefore, regard the reformers as outcastes. If untouchability was a part of the Hindu creed, I should decline to call myself a Hindu and most decidedly embrace some other faith if it satisfied my highest aspirations. Fortunately for me, I hold that untouchability is no part of Hinduism. On the contrary, it is a serious blot upon it, which every lover of it must sacrifice himself to remove. Suppose, however, I discover that untouchability was really an integral part of Hinduism, I should have to wander in the wilderness because the other creeds, as I know them through their accepted interpreters, would not satisfy my highest aspirations.

My correspondent accuses me of the crime of using the ambiguous middle in that I have confused Truth and non-violence with the Hindu creed. The crime is deliberate. It is the good fortune or the misfortune of Hinduism that it has no official creed. In order, therefore, to protect myself against any misunderstanding, I have said Truth and non-violence is my creed. If I were asked to define the Hindu creed, I should simply say: search after Truth through non-violent means. A man may not believe even in God and still call himself a Hindu. Hinduism is a relentless pursuit after truth and, if today it has become moribund, inactive, irresponsive to growth, it is because we are fatigued, and as soon as the fatigue is over, Hinduism will burst forth upon the world with brilliance perhaps unknown before. Of course, therefore, Hinduism is the most tolerant of all religions. Its creed is all-embracing. But to claim that is to claim superiority for the Hindu creed over all the other creeds of the world. As I write these lines, I feel a crowd of sectarians whispering to me, "That is no Hinduism you are defining, come to us and we will show you the Truth". I am confounding all these whisperers by saying not that, 'not that, my friends, not that,' and they make confusion worse confounded by retorting with redoubled fury, not that, not that.' But still another voice whispers to me, "Why all this duelling-this war of words? I can show you a way out of it. It lies through silent prayer." For the moment I propose to listen to that voice and observe silence and ask my friends to do likewise. Possibly I have failed to convince them and their co-sharers in their opinion. If I have failed to con-vines, it is because I have not seen the light. I can give my assurance that I have not indulged in special pleading in order to defend Maulana Mahomed Ali. If I discover my error, I hope I shall have the courage to own it. The Maulana needs no defence from me. And I should be a false friend if, in order to defend him, I sacrificed an iota of truth. It is the special privilege of a friend to own the other's faults and re-declare his affection in spite of faults.

❍

CHAPTER-4

Hinduism of Today

A correspondent styling himself *Sanatani* Hindu' writes: Hinduism of today presents many a curious anomaly. No one cares to study it, excepting perhaps some European missionaries...

"There is no definite body of doctrines or practices which may be called *sanatana* and should be respected.

A Sudra's status in a province where the Brahmins eat meat or fish is different from that in any province where the Brahmins and Vaishnavas alike refrain from meat or fish. You have somewhere said: "If you have no objection to drinking clean water given by a Sudra, you should have religious scruples against having water at the hands of meat-eaters, some against doing so at the hands of beef-eaters"..., I wish you could call a meeting of the untouchables of the whole province and take promises from them to abstain from beef or carrion as a preliminary to their being taken into the Hindu fold.

The letter presents only one side of the case. There is a reason for the correspondent's complaint. But Hinduism is a living organism liable to growth and decay, and subject to the laws of Nature. One and indivisible at the root, it has grown into a vast tree with innumerable branches. The changes in the seasons affect it. It has its autumn and summer, its winter and spring. The rains nourish and fructify it too. It is and is not based on scriptures. It does not derive its authority from one book. The *Gita is* universally accepted, but even then it only shows the way. It has hardly any effect on custom. Hinduism is like the Ganges, pure and unsullied at its source, but taking in its course the impurities in the way. Even like the Ganges it is beneficent in its total effect. It takes a provincial form in every province, but the inner substance is retained everywhere. Custom is not religion. Custom may change, but religion will remain unaltered.

Purity of Hinduism depends on the self-restraint of its votaries. Whenever their religion has been in danger, the Hindus have undergone rigorous penance, searched the causes of the danger and devised means for combating them. The Shastras are ever-growing. The Vedas, Upanishads, Smritis, Puranas, and Itihasas did not arise at one and the same time. Each grew out of the necessities of particular periods, and therefore they seem to conflict with one another. These books do not enunciate anew the eternal truths but show how these were practised at the time to which the books belong. A practice which was good enough in a particular period would, if blindly repeated in another, land people into the 'slough of despond'. Because the practice of animal-sacrifice obtained at one time, shall we revive it today? Because at one time, we used to eat beef, shall we revive it today? Because at one time, we used to chop off the hands and the feet of thieves, shall we revive that barbarity today? Shall we revive polyandry? Shall we revive child- marriages? Because we discarded a section of humanity one day, shall we brand their descendants today as outcastes?

Hinduism abhors stagnation. Knowledge is limitless and so also the application of truth. Everyday we add our knowledge of the power of *atman*, and we shall keep on doing so. New experience will teach us new duties, but truth shall ever be the same. Who has ever known it in its entirety? The Vedas represent the truth, they are infinite. But who has known them in their entirety? What has ever been known in its entirety? What goes today by the name of the Vedas is not even a millionth part of the real Veda-the Book of Knowledge. And who knows the entire meaning of even the few books that we have? Rather than wade through these infinite complications, our sages taught us to learn one thing: "As with the self, so with the Universe." It is not possible to scan the universe, as it is to scan the self. Know the self and you know the Universe. But even knowledge of the self within presupposes ceaseless striving-not only ceaseless but pure, and pure striving presupposes a pure heart, which in its turn depends on the practice *yamas* and *niyamas*-the cardinal and causal virtues.

This practice is not possible without God's grace which presupposes Faith and Devotion. This is why Tulsidas sang of the glory of *Ramanama*, that is why the author of the *Bhagavata* taught the *dwadashamantra (Om Nam Bhagavate Vasudevaya)*. To my mind, he is a sanatani Hindu who can repeat this mantra from the heart. All else is a bottomless pit, as the sage Akho has said.

But to come to the other part of the letter. The Europeans do study our manners and customs. But theirs is the study of a critic, not the study of a devotee. Their 'study' cannot teach me religion.

Boycott of beef-eaters may have been proper in the past. It is improper and impossible today. If you want the so-called untouchables to give up beef you can do only by means of love, only by quickening their intellects, not by despising them. Non-violent efforts to wean them away from their bad habits are going on, but Hinduism does not consist in eating and not-eating. Its kernel consists in right conduct, in correct observance of truth and non-violence. Many a man eating meat, but observing the cardinal virtues of compassion and truth, and living in the fear of God, is a better Hindu than a hypocrite who abstains from meat. And he whose eyes are opened to the truth of the violence in beef-eating or meat-eating and who has therefore rejected them, who 'loves both man and bird and beast' is worthy of our adoration. He has seen and known God: he is His best devotee. He is the teacher of mankind.

Hinduism and all other religions are being weighed in the balance. Eternal truth is one. God is one. Let everyone of us steer clear of conflicting creeds and customs and follow the straight path of truth. Only then shall we be true Hindus. Many styling themselves *sanatanis* stalk the earth. Who knows how few of them will be chosen by God! God's grace shall descend on those who do His will and wait upon Him, not on those who simply mutter "Ram Ram".

CHAPTER-5

Is There Satan in Hinduism?

A correspondent writes:

> "A few months back under a heading not quite justified by its contents you published a letter of mine concerning certain religious systems and the belief in God. Now I am tempted to put you a question concerning his adversary (according to Semitic beliefs), whose name you are so often using in your writings and speeches, not of course without effect, as witness the article "Snares of Satan" in your issue of 6-8-1925. If it was only rhetorical effect that was intended there-by, because you were writing or speaking in the language of a people who have been taught to believe in Satan's existence through the Semitic creed of Christianity, then I would have nothing to say. But the article cited, among other things, does seem to point to a belief on your part in Satan's existence, a belief, in my humble opinion, quite un-Hindu. Asked by Arjuna what was the cause of man's continual fall, Sri Krishna said: "*Kama esha, krodha esha*", etc. ("It is lust, it is anger"). According to Hindu belief, it would seem, the Tempter is no person outside of us, nor indeed is it one; for there are "the six enemies' of man enumerated in the Shastras: *kama* or lust, *krodha* or anger, *lobha* or greed, *moha* or infatuation, *maya* or pride, and *mat-sara*, i.e., envy or jealousy. So it is clear, Hinduism has no place for Satan, the Fallen Angel, the Tempter, or as he has been called by a French writer (Anatole France), 'God's- man-of-affairs'! How is it then that you who are a Hindu speak and write as if you believed in the real existence of the Old One?"

This correspondent is well known to the readers of *Young India*. He is too wide awake not to know the sense in which I could use the word Satan. But I have observed in him a disposition to draw me out on many matters about which there is a likelihood of the slightest misunderstanding or about which a greater elucidation may be considered necessary. In my opinion, the beauty of Hinduism lies in its all-embracing inclusiveness. What the divine author of the 'Mahabharata' said of his great creation is equally true of Hinduism. What of substance is contained in any other religion always to be found in Hinduism. And what is not contained in it is insubstantial or unnecessary. I do believe that there is room for Satan in Hinduism. The Biblical conception is neither new nor original. Satan is not a personality even in the Bible. Or he is as much a personality in the Bible as Ravana or the whole brood of the Asuras is in Hinduism. I no more believe in a historical Ravana with ten heads and twenty arms than in a historical Satan. And even as Satan and his companions are fallen angels, so are Ravana and his companion's fallen angels or call them gods, if you will. If it be a crime to clothe evil passions and ennobling thoughts in personalities, it is a crime for which perhaps Hinduism is the most responsible. For are not the six passions referred to by my correspondent, and nameless others, embodied in Hinduism? Who or what is Dhritarashtra and his hundred sons? To the end of time imagination, that is, poetry will play a useful and necessary part in the human evolution. We shall continue to talk of passions as if they were persons. Do they not torment us as much as evil persons? Therefore, as in innumerable other things, in the matter under notice the letter killeth, the spirit giveth life.

CHAPTER-6

Two Lectures on Hinduism

Mr M.K. Gandhi delivered the first of a series of lectures on Hinduism at the Masonic Temple, Plein Street, Johannesburg, under the auspices of the Johannesburg Lodge of the Theosophical Society. Major Peacock, vice-president, was in the chair.

Mr. Gandhi introduced his subject by remarking that the endeavours of the Johannesburg Lodge to promote interest in the study of different religious systems were most praiseworthy, tending as they did, to widen people's sympathies, and enlarge their comprehension of the motives and beliefs underlying the actions of those who were strangers in creed and colour. He himself had endeavoured, during his eleven years' residence in South Africa, to remove the prejudice and ignorance that Existed concerning his own people.

Continuing, the lecturer described what was meant by the title "Hindu", referring it to the branch of the Aryan people that had migrated to the trans-Indu-districts of India, and had colonized that vast country. As a matter of fact, Aryanism would have been a better descriptive word than Hinduism, in explanation of the faith accepted by so many millions of his countrymen.

One of the most remarkable characteristics of the religion professed by Hindus was self-abnegation, and this was obviously shown in the name of the religion itself, for, unlike most of the great world religions, it did not derive its name from any prophet or teacher, although it counted some of the greatest within its fold. The lecturer further instanced the historic siege of Arcot in support of this Contention, when the Indian soldiers, at a time when starvation faced the whole British Army, waived their claim to the rice rations in favour of the British soldiers, they themselves being content to have the water in which the rice had been boiled, although it was customary to throw this water away; and also the case of Prabhu Singh, an indentured British Indian, who was chosen for the post of honour of warning the inhabitants of Lady Smith during the siege, whenever a Boer shell was coming, by ringing a bell while perched in a tree, at imminent risk to himself. This man was mentioned several times in despatches by Sir George White.

The Hindus themselves claimed that the date of their scriptures was veiled in the midst of antiquity, the scriptures themselves being God-given. As against that, some Europeans contended that the scriptures were not more than 3,000 or 4,000 years old. Mr Tilak a well-known Indian Sanskritist, has, however, calculated that, from certain astronomical observations made in these works, they were at least 10,000 years old, although they were only committed to writing some three hundred years after Christ. The Vedas, as these scriptures were known, consisted of separate hymns, each being held to cover a definite period, and quite independent of each other. And typically, not one author's name had passed down to posterity. The Vedas had inspired the thought of many illustrious men of the West, amongst whom might be mentioned Arthur Schopenhauer and Professor Max Muller.

Over two hundred millions of people professed Hinduism, and this faith entered into their every act. The key-note of Hinduism on the spiritual side was *moksha*, or salvation; that is, the final absorption of the Soul in the Infinite Soul that pervades all things. In regard to religion, pantheism was the chief characteristic, whilst, on the ethical plane, self-abnegation was the most notable quality, with its corollary, toleration. In social matters, the characteristic of caste was predominant, whilst the ceremonial characteristic was the sacrificing of animals. At a time when the faith of the Hindus had become more formal, Prince Gautama Buddha having learnt the spiritual worth of things during a prolonged period of contemplation, commenced to teach that animal sacrifices were de-spiritualizing, and that the highest form of love was expressed by extending that toleration, which was already a tenet of their faith, in the direction of refraining from killing or otherwise destroying living things. Hinduism had never, as a religion, been missionary, as were Christianity and Mahomedanism, but, under King Asoka, the Buddhist priests were sent far and wide to propagate the new belief. Buddhism had a reforming effect upon Hinduism, somewhat similar to that of Protestantism upon Catholicism, but there was a great difference in the spirit underlying that reform. No Hindu bore the Buddhist any ill-will, a statement that could not be made in reference to the Protestants and Catholics. Buddhism was sometimes said to have declined in India. This was not really so. The Buddhist priests had endeavoured to propagate their faith too jealously, and had aroused the jealousy, at the time of the Hindu priesthood, who had driven the Buddhists to the outskirts of the country, to Tibet, China, Japan, Burma, and Ceylon. But the spirit of the Buddhists remained in India, and actuated every principle professed by the Hindus.

In this connection, the lecturer briefly referred to Jainism as a most interesting form of faith. The Jains claimed that it was altogether independent of Buddhism, not a growth from it. Unlike others, they did not claim for the faith that it was of Divine origin, recognizing that its sacred writings were the results of human workmanship. Jainism was, perhaps the most logical of faiths, and its most remarkable characteristic was its scrupulous regard for all things that lived.

Second Lecture

The lecturer, after giving a short resume of the previous lecture, said that the second lecture would be devoted to what might be termed the second epoch of Hinduism. After the reformation that took place from within, under the influence of the teachings of Buddha, Hinduism was very largely addicted to idolatry. Several explanations were offered in extenuation, but the lecturer could not deny the fact that the Hindus seemingly worshipped stocks and stones. The Hindu philosophers easily recognised and worshipped God as the purest spirit, and pantheism took them to the highest flight. It similarly, brought down the ignorant masses to the lowest depths. If the infant mind could not realise God as a pure spirit, it had no difficulty in worshipping Him through His various manifestations. Many worship him through the sun, the moon and the stars, and many worship him through stocks and icons also, a mode of worship to which philosophical Hinduism, with its tolerant spirit, had no difficulty in reconciling itself. So the wheel of Hindu life went merrily on, until there arose in the desert of Arabia a power that was destined to revolutionize ideas and to leave a permanent impress. Mahomet, whilst yet a boy on seeing around him people given to idolatry, to lustful indulgences, and to drunkenness, burned within himself with rage. He saw also Judaism prostrate and Christianity debased. He felt, even as did Moses and Christ, that he was a man with a mission. He decided to deliver his mission to the world, and he chose the members of his own family as the first recipients. The lecturer was not one of those who believed that the religion of Islam was a religion of the sword. Washington Irving, in his work on Islam, had asked a pertinent question, namely, "Where had Islam, in its first stage, found men to wield the sword?" He believed that the success of Mahomedanism was largely due to its simplicity and to its recognition of human weaknesses. He (the Prophet) taught that God was One and only One, that he was His Messenger. He taught also that prayer was absolutely necessary as an uplifting influence, and in order to bring together his followers, if only once in a year, he instituted the pilgrimage to Mecca, for those who could afford it, and recognizing that people would amass wealth, he enjoined upon his followers that they set apart a certain portion of it religiously, for charitable purposes. The key-note of Islam was, however, its levelling spirit. It offered equality to all that came within its pale, in the manner that no other religion in the world did. When therefore, about 900 years after Christ, his followers descended it. (The doctrine of equality could not but appeal to the masses that were caste-ridden.) To this inherent strength was also added the power of the sword. The fanatical raiders, who, from time to time, found their way into India, did not hesitate to convert by the sword if they could not do so by persuasion. They more or less overran all parts of India, breaking idols, and although the Rajput was at the disposal of Hinduism, it was powerless to afford protection against the Mahomedan in-road. In keeping with the spirit of Hinduism, an attempt was made at first to bring about reconciliation between the two faiths, and in the city of Benares, there arose a holy man about the 13th century, by name Kabir, who endeavoured, by keeping intact the chief tenets of Hinduism and by borrowing somewhat from Mahomedanism, to bring about a fusion, but the attempt was not quite successful. The Punjab, through which the Mahomedan conquerors poured into India, and which bore the first brunt, produced Guru Nanak, the founder of the Sikh religion, who drew upon Kabir for his doctrines and added to it militant Hinduism. He offered the olive-branch by respecting the Moslem susceptibilities, but if that were not accepted, he was equally ready to defend Hinduism from the Moslem aggression, and thus Sikhism was a direct result of Islam. It was well known how brave the Sikh was and what the effect of Mahomedanism on Hinduism was that it gave rise to Sikhism and it brought out one of the chief characteristics of the religion, namely toleration in its true light and fullness. When there were no political influences at work, there was no difficulty about the Hindus and the Mahomedans prejudices of the other, and each following his own faith without lot or hindrance. It was Hinduism that gave Mahomedanism its Akbar, who with unerring insight, recognized the tolerant spirit and adopted it himself in ruling India. Hinduism, moreover, showed its elasticity in that; in spite of the fierce struggle, the classes, as well as large majority of the masses, were left totally untouched, and Hinduism arose out of the struggle backed as we would rise out of a cold bath, with warm glow. The first shock was, no doubt, severely felt, but the Hindu religion soon asserted itself. The lecturer also mentioned the Fakirs and the Yogis, and said that they lived almost the same kind of life, although the former belonged to the Islamic faith and the latter to the Hindu faith.

At the end of the lecture several interesting questions were put, and the proceedings terminated after the usual vote of thanks.

CHAPTER-7

The Hindus

Hindus are not considered to be the original inhabitants of India. According to Western scholars, the Hindus, as well as most of the European people, lived at one time in Central Asia. Migrating from there some went to Europe, some to Iran, others moved south-eastwards down into India through the Punjab, and there spread the Aryan religion. The Hindu population in India exceeds two hundred million. They are called Hindus because they once lived beyond the river Sindhu (Indus). The Vedas are their oldest scripture Very devout Hindus believe that the Vedas are of divine origin and without beginning. Western scholars hold these were composed before 2000 B.C. The famous Mr Tilak of Poona has shown that the Vedas must be at least 10,000 years old. The main thing that distinguishes the Hindus is their belief that the *brahman* or oversoul is all-pervading. What we all have to attain is *moksha* or liberation, *moksha* here meaning freeing oneself from the evil of birth and death and merging in the *brahman* Humility and even-mindedness are the chief qualities of their ethics; while caste reigns supreme in their temporal affairs.

The Hindu religion underwent its first trial on the advent of Lord Buddha. The Buddha was himself the king. He is said to have been born before 600 B.C. At that time the Hindus were under the glamour of the outward form of their religion, and the Brahmins had, out of selfishness, abandoned their true function of defending the Hindu faith. Lord Buddha was, moved to-pity when he saw his religion reduced such a plight. He renounced the world and started doing penance. He spent several years in devout contemplation and ultimately suggested some reform in the Hindu religion. His piety greatly affected the minds of the Brahmins, and the killing of animals for sacrifice was stopped to a great extent. It cannot, therefore, be said that the Buddha founded a new or different religion. But those who came after him gave his teachings the identity of a separate religion. King Ashoka the Great sent missionaries to different lands for the propagation of Buddhism, and spread that religion in Ceylon, China, Burma and other countries. A distinctive beauty of Hinduism was revealed during this process: no one was converted to Buddhism by force. People's minds were sought to be influenced only by discussion and argument and mainly by the very pure conduct of the preachers themselves. It may be said that, in India at any rate, Hinduism and Buddhism were but one, and that even today the fundamental principles of both are identical.

We have seen that Buddhism had a salutary effect on Hinduism, that the champions of the latter were aroused by its impact. A thousand years ago, the Hindu religion came under another influence more profound. Hazrat Mahomed was born 1300 years ago. He saw moral anarchy rampant in Arabia. Judaism was struggling for survival; Christianity was not able to gain a foothold in the land; and the people were given to licence and self-indulgence. Mahomed felt all this to be improper. It caused him mental agony; and in the name of God, he determined to make them realise their miserable condition. His feeling was so intense that he was able immediately to impress the people around him with his fervour, and Islam spread very rapidly. Zeal or passion, then, is a great specialty, a mighty force, of Islam. It has been the cause of many good deeds, and sometimes of bad ones too. A thousand years ago the army of Ghazni invaded India in order to spread Islam. Hindu idols were broken and the invasions advanced as far as Somnath. While, on the other, unfolding the real merit of Islam- the Islamic principle that all those who embraced Islam were equals made such a favourable impression on the lower classes that hundreds of thousands of Hindus accepted that faith, and there was great commotion in the whole community.

Kabir was born in Banares. He thought that, according to Hindu philosophy, there could be no distinction between a Hindu and a Muslim. Both of them, if they did good works, would find a place in heaven. Idolatry was not an essential part of Hinduism. Reasoning thus, he attempted to bring about a synthesis between Hinduism and Islam; but it did not have much effect, and he became no more than a distinct sect, and it exists even today. Some years later, Guru Nanak was born in the Punjab; he accepted the reasoning of Kabir and made a similar attempt to fuse the two religions. But while doing so, he felt that Hinduism should be defended against Islam, if necessary with the sword. This gave rise to Sikhism, and produced the Sikh warriors. The result of all this is that, despite the prevalence of Hinduism and Islam as the two principal religions of India today, both the communities live together in peace and amity and are considerate enough not to hurt one another's feelings save for the bitterness caused by political machinations and excitement. There is very little difference between a Hindu yogi and a Muslim fakir.

While Islam and Hinduism were thus vying with each other, the Christians landed at the port of Goa about 500 years ago, and set about converting Hindus to Christianity. They also partly resorted to force and (converted) partly through persuasion. Some of their ministers were exceedingly tender-hearted and kind, rather one would call them saintly. Like the fakirs they made a deep impression on the lower classes of Hindu society. But later, when Christianity and Western civilization came to be associated, the Hindus began to look upon that religion with disfavour. And today, we see few Hindus embracing Christianity in spite of the fact that the Christians are ruling over a vast kingdom. Nevertheless, Christianity has had a very considerable influence on Hinduism. Christian priests imparted education of a high order and pointed out some of the glaring defects in Hinduism, with the result that there arose 'among the Hindus other great teachers, who like Kabir, began to teach the Hindus what was good in Christianity and appealed to them to remove these defects. To this category belonged Raja Ram Mohan Rai, Devendranath Tagore, and Keshab Chandra Sen. In Western India we had Dayanand Saraswati. And the numerous reformist associations like the Brahmo Samaj and the Arya Samaj that have sprung up in India today are doubtless the result of Christian influence. Again, Madame Blavatsky came to India, told both Hindus and the Muslims of evils of Western civilization and asked them to beware of becoming enamoured of it.

Thus, we have seen how there have been three assaults on Hinduism, coming from Buddhism, Islam and then Christianity, but how on the whole it came out of them unscathed. It has tried to imbibe whatever was good in each of these religions. We should, however, know what the followers of this religion, Hinduism, believe. This is what they believe: God exists. He is without beginning, immaculate, and without any attribute or form. He is omnipresent and omnipotent. His original form is *Brahman* It neither does, nor causes to be done. It does not govern. It is bliss incarnate, and by it all this is sustained. The soul exists, and is distinct from the body. It also is without a beginning, without birth. Between its original form and the *Brahman*, there is no distinction. But it takes on, from time to time a body as a result of *karma* or the power of *maya*, and goes on being born again and again into high or low species in accordance with the good or bad deeds performed by it. To be free from the cycle of birth and death and be merged in *Brahman* is *moksha* or liberation. The way to achieve this *moksha* is to do pure and good deeds; to have compassion for all living beings, and to live in truth. Even after reaching this stage, one does not attain liberation, for one has to enjoy embodied existence as a consequence of one's good deeds as well. One has, therefore, to go a step further. We will, however, have to continue to act, only we should not cherish any attachment to our actions. Action should undertake for its own sake, without an eye on the fruit. In short, everything should be dedicated to God. We should not cherish, even in a dream, the feeling of pride that we do or can do anything. We should look upon all equally. These are the beliefs or tenets of Hinduism, but there admittedly exist a number of schools. Also, there have arisen a few factions or sects resulting from (differences in) secular practices. But we need not consider them on the present occasion.

If, after listening to this, any one of you has been favourably impressed and has come to feel that the Hindus or the Indians, in whose country the religion expounded above prevails, cannot be altogether an inferior people, you can render service to my countrymen even without becoming involved in political matters.

All religions teach that we should all live together in love and mutual kindness. It was not my intention to preach you a sermon neither I am fit to do so. But if it has produced any favourable impression on your mind, I would appeal to you to let my brethren have its benefit and, as behoves the English people, to defend them, whenever they are maligned.

Sanatana Hindu

I have a correspondent who always brings me to book for the slightest negligence on my part. He is evidently a regular student of *Young India,* but no blind admirer. Here is a candid but friendly critic, and, if he sees something good in my writings, he detects errors also. One of his letters drawing attention to a possible inconsistency in my writings has long remained in file. One portion of it deals with the definition of '*Sanatana Hindu*'. Here is the letter:

"You have often declared yourself a sanatana Hindu, defining one as a believer in the Vedas, Smritis etc., and laid emphasis on the institution of castes by birth as legitimately following from the 'scriptures'. Of course, you limit the number of castes to the supposed pristine four. (I say 'supposed pristine' advisedly; for, even as early as the times of the production of Manu('s) and other Smritis, there had been already so many castes evolved out of and recognized over and above the ideal four, although, be it noted, inter-dining and intermarriage amongst them all had not yet come to be interdicted.) Now the fourth or, last in order of the "fundamental' castes, is the *Sudra*, which is debarred by those very 'scriptures' a belief in which you regard as the *sine qua* non of a *sanatana* Hindu, as well as by their 'twice-born' professors, from studying or reciting the Divine Vedas including the *Gayatri*, a recitation of which you mention as obligatory upon a *Sanatana* Hindu (without distinction of caste). So the question arises: How can anyone (e.g., a *Sudra*) be said to belong to a religion (*viz.*, Hinduism as defined by you), if the mere reading, reciting or even the hearing of its scripture is tabooed to him, as though it were a sacrilege? How can you expect a man to be a swimmer without letting him step into water? Either one who is born a Sudra cannot be a *sanatana* Hindu in your sense, or else a *sanatana* Hindu must be something very different from what you define one to be. (I refer you to your old article on 'Hinduism' in 1921 and your address to the cow conference at Belgaum as printed in *Young India*, 29-1-1925). I for one, whom a Brahmin birth, cannot glorify in the name of 'Hindu' so long as an exemplar of real *sanatana dharma* like you permits the term to cover a bundle of contradictions like the one I have pointed out. Lastly, in view of your mention of *Gayatri*, may I humbly inquire whether you have in your 'twice-born' life never omitted to include the *Gayatri* in your daily prayers?"

I am not a literalist. Therefore, I try to understand the spirit of the various scriptures of the world. I apply the test of Truth and Ahimsa laid down by these very scriptures for interpretation. I reject what is; inconsistent with that test, and I appropriate all that is consistent with it. The story of a Sudra having been punished by Ramachandra for daring to learn the Vedas I reject as an interpolation. And in any event, I worship Rama, the perfect being of my conception, not a historical person, facts about whose life may vary with the progress of new historical discoveries and researches. Tulsidas had nothing to do with the Rama of history. Judged by historical test, his Ramayana would be fit for the scrap heap. As a spiritual experience, his book is almost unrivalled, at least for me. And then, too, I do not swear by every word that is to be found in so many editions published as the *Ramayana* of Tulsidas. It is the spirit running through the book that holds me spell-bound. I cannot myself subscribe to the prohibition against Sudras learning the Vedas. Indeed, in my opinion, at the present moment, we are all predominantly Sudras as long as we are serfs. Knowledge cannot be the prerogative of any class or section. But I can conceive the impossibility of people assimilating higher or subtler truths, unless they have undergone preliminary training, even as those who have not made preliminary preparations are quite unfit to breathe the rarefied atmosphere in high altitudes, or those who have no preliminary training in simple mathematics are unfit to understand or assimilate higher geometry are algebra. Lastly, I believe in certain healthy conventions. There is a convention surrounding the recitation of the *Gayatri*. The convention is that it should be recited only at stated times and after ablutions performed in the prescribed manner. As I believe in those conventions, and as I am not able always to conform to them, for years past I have followed the later Saints, and therefore have satisfied myself with the *Dwadasha Mantra* of the *Bhagavata* or the still simpler formula of Tulsidas and a' few selections from the Gita and other works, and a few *bhajans* in Prakrit. These are my daily spiritual food-my *Gayatri*. They give me all the peace and solace I need from day-to-day.

Who is a Sanatani Hindu?

It has been asked why I call myself an orthodox *sanatani* Hindu and why I regard myself as a *Vaishnava*. I think I should answer these questions.

The answer will cover the definition of a *sanatani* Hindu and include a complete description of a *Vaishnava*.

According to my belief, a Hindu is anyone who, born in a Hindu family in India, accepts the Vedas, the Upanishads and the Puranas as holy books; who has faith in the five *Yamas* of truth, non-violence, etc., and practices them to the best of his ability; who believes in the existence of the *atman* and the *Paramatma*, and believes, further, that the *atman* is never born and never dies but, through incarnation in the body passes from existence to existence and is capable of attaining *moksha*; who believes that *moksha* is the supreme end of human striving and believes in *varnashrama* and cow-protection. Whoever, besides believing in all these, has been born in a family belonging to the *Vaishnava* sect and has not forsaken the *Vaishnava* way; who possesses in some measure the qualities described in Narasinh Mehta's devotional song entitled "*Vaishnava-jana*" and strives to cultivate these qualities in perfection is a *Vaishnava*. It is my firm belief that I possess in a large measure the characteristics described by me and I have been striving to strengthen them. I do not, therefore, hesitate to call myself with all firmness, though humbly, a strict *sanatani* Hindu and a *Vaishnava*. I believe that the most important outward form of Hinduism is cow-protection. I regard the Hindu world as impotent because at present not a single Hindu is capable of giving that protection. Among these impotent people, I believe myself to be the least impotent. I do not believe that there can be anybody else who has systematically exerted himself as much as I have done, and am still doing, for the protection of cows or who feels for the cow and its progeny as much as I do. As long as the Hindus in India show no kindness to the cow, as long as they themselves torture cattie in many ways, as long as they have not succeeded in winning the regard of Muslims and persuading them to stop, out of their regard, the slaughter of cows, and as long as they tolerate the killing of cows by the English and salute the British flag, I shall believe that the Brahmin and the Kshatriya spirit has vanished from Hinduism. Therefore, though born a Vaisya, I am ever active in the duties of both.

I believe that the essence of Hinduism is truth and non-violence. I have not seen anyone among those whom I know respecting truth as scrupulously as I have been doing right from my childhood. The active manifestation of non-violence is love-absence of ill-will. I firmly believe that I am overflowing with love. I have not felt ill will against anyone even in a dream. I entertain no such feeling towards Dyer, his wicked deeds notwithstanding. Wherever I have seen misery or injustice, I have felt troubled in my soul.

The central principle of Hinduism is that of *moksha*. I am ever striving for it. All my activities are for *moksha*. I have as much faith in the existence of the *atman* and in its immortality as I am certain of the existence of my body and its transience.

For these reasons, I am happy to declare myself a staunch *sanatani* Hindu.

If anybody asks me whether I have made any deep study of the Shastra's, I would say that I have and I have not. I have not studied them from a *scholar's* point of view. My knowledge of Sanskrit is almost nil. Even of the translations available in modem Indian languages, I have read only a few. I cannot claim to have fully read even a single Veda. Nevertheless, I have understood the *shastras* from the point of view of *dharma*. I have grasped their real meaning. I know that one can attain *moksha* without reading the Vedas.

I have found the right method for reading—for understanding— the *shastras*. If any injunction in a *shastra is* opposed to truth, nonviolence and *brahmacharya*, it is unauthentic, whichever the *shastra* in which it is found. The *shastras* are not above reason. We can reject any *shastras* which reason cannot follow. I have read through only the Upanishads. I have also read some among them which my reason cannot follow. I did not, therefore, accept them as having any authority. Many poets have told us in their poems that anyone who sticks to the letter of the *shastras* is a pedant, Teachers like Shankaracharya have given the essence of the *shastras* in single sentences, and the sum and substance of it all is that one should cultivate *bhakti* towards God and attain *jnana*, and thereby attain *moksha*. Akha Bhagat has said: Live as you please.

Attain God anyhow, somehow.

That *shastra* which teaches me drinking liquor, eating meat and wicked ways cannot be called a *shastra*. Much that is the very opposite of *dharma* is going on in the name of the *smritis*. By trying to follow the letter of the *smritis* and other such works, we make ourselves fit for hell. Deluded by these, people who call themselves Hindus give themselves up to licence and become ready to commit or make others commit sin on young girls.

We now have before us the important question of what, in all the *shastras*, we should regard as interpolations, what is acceptable and what as deserving to be rejected. If there had not been, as I have stated above, a total extinction of the Brahmin spirit, we could have consulted a Brahmin who had purified himself by following the disciplines of *yamaniyama* and acquired a good measure of *jnana*. In the absence of such Brahmins, the path of *bhakti* rules supreme at present. When we have brought about self-purification by non-cooperating with the present Government in which the sins of hypocrisy, pretension, pride, worldliness and so on, reveal themselves in numerous ways, then perhaps we shall get a cultured person who can give us the essence of the *shastras*.

Till then we, the common people, may cling to the essentials with a simple faith and live our lives in *bhakti* to God. I see no other way.

"There can be no *jnana* without a guru" is a golden maxim. But it is very difficult to find a guru, and it would not be proper to accept any person as a guru in the absence of a good one and so drown ourselves right in the middle of our voyage across. How can a man who knows no swimming save others? Even if such swimmers exist in modern times, they are not a common sight.

Let us now examine *varnashrama*. I have always believed that there are no more than four *varnas*. I believe that one acquires one's caste by birth. One who is born in a Brahmin family dies a Brahmin. If he becomes a non-Brahmin through his qualities of character, his Brahmin body does not cease to be such. A Brahmin who does not follow the Brahmin *dharma* may be born, according to his deserts, as a Sudra, or even as an animal. A Vaisya like me who follows the dharma of a Brahmin and of a Kshatriya, if he has to be born again, may well be a Brahmin or a Kshatriya in the next birth. So far as this life is concerned, he will remain but a Vaisya, and rightly so. From time to time persons belonging to other faiths have been absorbed by Hinduism, but they were not known as Hindus during their lifetime. The Hindu world is like a sea. All refuse that finds its way into its bosom gets purified, settles down. This has happened again and again. People from Italy, Greece and elsewhere came in and were absorbed by Hinduism, but they were not converted by anyone to Hinduism. Merely in course of ages, the numbers have risen and fallen. Unlike Christianity or Islam, Hinduism does not invite persons of other faiths to join its fold; it enjoins all to follow their own religions. Sister Nivedita, for instance, embraced Hinduism but we do not think of her as a Hindu, nor do we boycott or slight her in any way. There is no question of anybody embracing Hinduism. Everybody can practise Hinduism.

Varnashrama is a law. The practical question is the caste system. Castes are subject to increase and decrease (in number). They come into existence and they disappear. Only the man himself can leave Hinduism, though he may be expelled from the caste. Excommunication by the caste is a mode of punishment and ought to be available to every community.

It is certainly necessary that the numerous castes should become fewer, and this can be brought about by the councils of the various castes without injury to Hinduism. If the various divisions of Banias were together and their members marry among themselves, that will not harm religion in any way.

The rules which people observe in regard to food, water and marriage are not essential features, of Hinduism but, because self-control has been given special importance in Hinduism, restrictions have been laid down, even to the smallest detail in regard to these matters. I do not think that they deserve to be condemned, but at the same time, I would not regard a person who does not observe them as having transgressed *dharma*. Not to have water or food or enter into matrimonial alliance anywhere and everywhere, I regard as civilized behaviour. This ensures preservation of health and purity. But I believe that not accepting food or water at anybody's place through contempt is opposed to Hinduism. It is my view, based on experience, that the prohibition as to dining with or marrying a person of another *varna* or another religion is as essential protective fence for its culture put up by Hinduism.

Why do I, then, dine even at the homes of Muslims? I do so because, even when dining with them, I am able to observe the utmost self-restraint. Among cooked articles, I go so far as to take bread, because the process of baking bread is absolutely clean and just as pop-corn can always be taken, no matter where roasted, similarly bread (not *rod*) can be taken wherever it may have been baked. But my co-workers do not observe even this restriction and eat any articles, otherwise acceptable, in the home of a Muslim or of a person belonging to a caste other, than their own, if the articles are prepared hygienically. In doing so, they run the risk of being expelled from their caste, but they do not cease to be Hindus. The *Ashram* follows a kind of *dharma* appropriated to *sannyasis*. There a new caste or a new code of conduct, suitable to the present age and in conformity with Hinduism, is being formed. I look upon this effort as an experiment. If it succeeds, it will be treated as worthy of adoption. If it fails, it will have harmed no one. Even those engaged in the experiment will not be harmed, because the basis of the experiment is self-control. The aim is to be able to carry on the work of service with ease and to see that unlike at present, when religion has come to-be confined to rules about eating and drinking, the conventions in those matters are kept in their proper and subordinate place.

Now remains the issue of untouchability. Nobody can trace the origin of this practice. I have merely ventured guesses. They may be right or wrong. But even a blind man can see that the practice of untouchability is contrary to *dharma*. Only, in the same way as the atman's inhabiting (the body) for ages prevents us from knowing it, the long existence of the practice of untouchability does not permit us to see the *adharma* inherent in it. To make any persons crawl on their stomachs, to segregate them, to drive them to live on the outskirts of the village, not to be concerned whether they live or die, to give them food left over by others-all this certainly cannot be religion. We are inflicting upon untouchables an outrage grosser than that in the Punjab against which we have been protesting. That an untouchable cannot live in our neighbourhood and cannot own land that an untouchable must, on seeing us, shout: "Please keep at a distance, do not touch me," and should not be permitted to sit with us in the train-this is not Hinduism. This is Dyerism. There is no self-control in the practice of untouchability. An analogy has been cited in justification of it, viz., that a mother, after removing stools, does not touch anything without taking a bath. But in this instance the mother herself does not wish to touch anything and, if we sought to enforce such a rule in respect of *Bhangis*, nobody will object. By treating *Bhangis* and others as untouchables, we only tolerate filth and breed diseases. If we look upon untouchables as touchables, we shall see to it that limb of ours remains clean.

I have found the homes of *Bhangis* for cleaner than many *Vaishnava* houses. I have been astonished at the truthfulness, simplicity, kindness and such other qualities in some of them. It is my conviction that we have fallen because of the entry into Hinduism of the demon of untouchability, and have, in consequence, also become powerless to ensure the protection of mother cow. So long as we have not rid ourselves of this Dyerism, we have no right to ask that we should be freed from the Dyerism of the British.

Duty of Hindus

I draw the attention of all Hindus to the touching letter given below which I have received from the Antyajashram at Godhra.

Every Hindu should hang his head in shame on reading this letter. We, arid not the boy's parents, are responsible for the beating which he got. We have despised Antyajas, given them our leftovers and rotten food to eat, persuading ourselves that we were doing a virtuous deed. We paid them as little as possible and drove them to begging. Not only have we made them carry our filth, but we have also made them eat filth. We have been giving them our discarded garments to serve as finery. The result is that the Antyajas now like begging and feel proud when they get leftovers. When parents return home with rotten grain, the children dance with joy. The master whose slaves rejoice in their slavery has sinned beyond measure. This is the position of the Hindus.

The child who got a beating for his reformed habits and for refusing to eat leftovers was our child. After reading this article, let all parents look at their children and ask themselves how they would feel if the latter were in the same plight as the other child. And how pure was that boy! Though beaten he refused to eat meat! What must be the mental condition of those who regard such a child as untouchable? Will they be able to enjoy *Swaraj*? Will they protect others?

At the moment, however, I do not wish to say anything about untouchability to the caste-Hindu parents. Will they not have even simple compassion on their "untouchable" brothers? Is it also in the Shastras to give them dirty, leftover food and pay them as little as possible? I request all parents:

1. not to give Antyajas cooked food;
2. to give them only uncooked grain;
3. not to give them garments of foreign cloth or worn-out and dirty clothes;
4. to raise their wages, if they are low; and
5. whatever they give, to give it with love.

I urge those Antyajas who may read this article to resolve that they will not accept or eat rotten grain or leftover food or meat and advise them to send their children to the national schools which may be started for them.

What may Hindu do?

I have received many communications on the Hindu-Muslim statement, but there being nothing new or striking in them, I have not published them. But I gladly print Babu Bhagwandas's letter and answer his questions.

Regarding the first two questions, the writer has answered them himself. In my opinion, they are only partly true. Though the majority of the Mussalmans of India and the Hindus belong to the same 'stock', the religious environment has made them different. I believe and I have noticed too that thought transforms man's features as well as character. The Sikhs are the most recent illustration of the fact. The Mussalman, being generally in a minority, has as a class developed into a bully. Moreover, being heir to fresh traditions, he exhibits the virility of a comparatively new system of life. Though, in my opinion, non-violence has a predominant place in the Koran, the thirteen hundred years of imperialistic expansion has made the Mussalmans fighters as a body. They are therefore aggressive. Bullying is the natural excrescence of an aggressive spirit. The Hindu has an ages-old civilization. He is essentially non-violent. His civilization has passed through the experiences that the two recent ones are still passing through. If Hinduism was ever imperialistic in the modern sense of the term, it has outlived its imperialism and has, either deliberately or as a matter of course, given it up. Predominance of the non-violent spirit has restricted the use of arms to a small minority which must always be subordinate to a civil power highly Spiritual, learned and selfless. The Hindus as a body are, therefore, not equipped for fighting. But not having retained their spiritual training, they have forgotten the use of an effective substitute for arms and, not knowing their use nor having an aptitude for them, they have become docile to the point of timidity of cowardice. This vice is, more, a natural excrescence of gentleness. Holding this view, I do not think that the Hindu exclusiveness, bad as it undoubtedly is, has much to do with the Hindu timidity. Hence, also, my disbelief in *akhadas* as a means of self-defence. I prize them for physical culture but, for self-defence, I would restore the spiritual culture. The best and most lasting self-defense is self-purification. I refuse to be lifted off my feet because of the scares that haunt us today. If Hindus would but believe in themselves and work in accordance with their traditions, they will have no reason to fear bullying. The moment they recommence the real spiritual training the Mussalman will respond. He cannot help it. If I can get together a band of young Hindus with faith in them and, therefore, faith in the Mussalmans, the band will become a shield for the weaker ones. They (the young Hindus) will teach how to die without killing. I know no other way. When our ancestors saw affliction surrounding them, they went in for *tapasya*-purification. They realized the helplessness of the flesh and in their helplessness they prayed till they compelled the Maker to obey their call. 'Oh yes,' says my Hindu friend, but then God sent someone to wield arms.' I am not concerned with denying the truth of the retort. All I say to the friend is that as a Hindu he may not ignore the cause and secure the result. It will be time to fight when we have done enough *tapasya*. Are we purified enough, I ask? Have we even done willing penance for the sin of untouchability, let alone the personal purity of individuals? Are our religious preceptors all that they should be? We are beating the air whilst we simply concentrate our attention upon picking holes in the Mussalman conduct. As with Englishmen, so with the Mussalman. If our professions are true, we should find it infinitely less difficult to conquer the Mussalman than the English. But Hindus whisper to me that they have hope of the Englishman but none of the Mussalman. I say to them, 'If you have no hope of the Mussalman, your hope of the Englishman is foredoomed to failure.'

The other questions can be briefly answered. The goondas came on the scene because the leaders wanted them. The leaders distrusted one another. Distrust never comes from well-defined causes. A variety of causes, more felt than realized, breeds distrust. We have not yet visualized the fact that our interests are identical. Each party seems vaguely to believe that it can displace the other by some land of manoeuvring. But I freely confess, as suggested by Babu Bhagwandas that our not knowing the kind of *swaraj* we want, has also a great deal to do with the distrust. I used not to think so, but he had almost converted me before I became Sir George Lloyd's guest at the Yeravda Central Prison. I am now a confirmed convert.

The 'points of contact' referred to by me is a phrase intended to cover all social, religious and political relations alike as between individuals and masses. Thus, for instance, instead of accentuating the differences in religion, I should set about discovering the good points common to both. I would bridge the social distance wherever I can do consistently with my religious belief. I would go out of my way to seek common ground on the political field.

As for the referee, I have named Hakim Saheb's name undoubtedly for the universal respect that it carried with it. But I would not hesitate to put the pen even in the hands of a Mussalman who may be known for his prejudices and fanaticism. For, as a Hindu, I should know that I have nothing to lose even if the referee gave the Mussalmans a majority of seats in every province. There is no principle at stake in giving or having seats in elective bodies. Moreover, experience has taught me to know that undivided responsibility immediately puts a man on his mettle and his pride or god fearingness sobers him.

Lastly, no proclamation or any such thing will avail unless some of us begin to act up to the proclamation even though we may be the fewest possible.

To Hindus

I see that the Hindus have still mental reservations about going all out to make sacrifices on the *khilafat* issue. I decided many years ago that India's good lay in unity of heart between Hindus and Muslims. That is why on the Satyagraha Day, i.e., April 5, special stress was laid on Hindu-Muslim unity.

I attach far more importance to Hindu-Muslim unity than to the British connection. This latter is not indispensable for the prosperity of India, whereas Hindu-Muslim unity is. Three-fourths of India can never enjoy freedom if they remain hostile to the remaining one-fourth. Extermination of seven crore Muslims is equally impossible.

Many Hindus believe that British rule serves at any rate to protect Hinduism, and, therefore, whatever other harms it may do, the protection of Hinduism is a sufficient compensation. I can think of no more humiliating idea which can occur to a Hindu. If twenty-three crore Hindus are not strong enough to defend themselves against seven crore Muslims, either the Hindu religion is false or those who believe in it are cowardly and wicked.

I would rather say that the Hindus and the Muslims settled their accounts by means of the sword than that the British Government maintained artificial peace between them.

If, however, we do not wish to fight it out with the Muslims, if we wish to live with them as with our own brothers, if we would ensure protection of cows, of our temples and our women by winning over their hearts and through a friendly approach, we should welcome the opportunity we have today. The like of it will not come, again for a hundred years.

It is wrong to believe that Muslims and Hindus can never get along together-. To be sure, you will find in history cases of injustice done by Muslims. But their religion is a noble one and Muslims are noble people. I do not believe that they have no respect for people of other faiths, or that they have no compassion in them. They know how to repay obligations. I, therefore, advise every Hindu to place full trust in his Muslim brethren. Man by nature is pure in his heart and Muslims are no exception to this law.

So far, we have made no sincere efforts to bring about unity. Such an attempt expects no reward. Sincerity is not a matter for a shop-keeper's calculations. To help Muslims on certain conditions is as good as not helping them. The hearts of seven crores cannot be changed by making conditions. Their trust and their respect can be won only by helping them in their time of need. Reward should be asked only of God. My Hindu religion teaches me not to expect a reward while doing any good deed and to trust that good always produces well. Knowing that this is an unalterable law, if we come across an instance which seems to contradict it, we should think that, with our limited understanding, we are unable to explain the contradiction. We have no ground for taking it to be an exception. God always puts man to a severe test. He helps him who does not forget Him in the direst adversity, i.e., who keeps up his faith in truth. That is why He has been called the Protector of the weak.

But suppose that Muslims betray Hindus despite the latter's generous behaviour. Will Hindus, in that case, remain cowards? Are they not strong enough to protect their religion? If Hindus want to acquire strength to protect their religion, this too they will acquire by helping Muslims because, in the process, Hindus will have to display the great qualities of determination, courage, truthfulness, capacity for self-sacrifice, unity, organizing ability, etc.

I do not mean that Hindus should help because of their own weakness, but rather that it has become our duty to help the Muslims as neighbours since their case is just and the means they are employing are also just. If they do not do this duty, they will strengthen their bonds of slavery and lose for ever the opportunity of winning the friendship of Muslims. Doing it, they will shake off slavery and win over Muslims.

Looking at the matter in this way, (we see that) it is the highest duty of every Hindu to help Muslims since, in doing so, he will be saving India and protecting his religion. There can be no thought of reward or fear in discharging such a duty. Bringing about so good and great a result requires a *yajna*-a supreme yajna. Offering up, in this *yajna*, our titles, our practice and our education for material gain is, in my opinion, but a small sacrifice. Whether the Hindus make this sacrifice or not, every Hindu should try and understand the true meaning of this war.

❍

CHAPTER-8

Varnashrama

The reader will find in another column Sjt. Nadkarni's interesting letter on the *Brahmiti-Non-Brahman* question. I gladly respond to his invitation to explain my views on *varnashrama* more fully than I have done in my speeches during the recent Tamilnadu tour, which have been more or less fully reproduced in these columns.

Let me clear the issue by dismissing from consideration the celebrated story of a Sudra said to have had his head cut off by Rama by reason of his having dared to become a *sannyasi*. I do not read Shastras literally, certainly not as history. The story of the decapitation of Shambuka is not in keeping with the general character of Rama. And whatever may be said in the various *Ramayanas*, I hold my Rama to be incapable of having decapitated a Sudra or for that matter anyone else. The story of Shambuka, if it proves anything, proves that in the days when the story arose it was held to be a capital crime for Sudras to perform certain rites. We are in the dark as to the meaning of the word Sudra here. I have heard even an allegorical meaning given to the whole version. But that would not alter the fact of certain unreasonable prohibitions operating against the Sudras at some stage in the evolution of Hinduism. Only I do not need to join Sjt. Nadkarni in doing penance for the alleged decapitation of Shambuka, for I do not believe in a historical person by that name having been decapitated by a historical person called Rama. For the general persecution of the so-called lower orders of Hinduism, especially the so-called untouchables, I am, as a Hindu, doing penance every moment of my life. In my opinion, illustrations like that of Shambuka have no place in a religious consideration of the question of *varnashrama*. I propose therefore-merely to say what I believe to be *varnashrama*, and I should not hesitate to reject the institution if it was proved to me that the interpretation put upon it by me has no warrant in Hinduism. *Varna* and *ashrama* are, as Sjt. Nadkarni says, two different words. The institution of four *ashramas* enables one the better to fulfill the purpose of life for which the law of *varna is* a necessity. The law of *varna* prescribes that a person should, for his living, follow the lawful occupation of his forefathers. I hold this to be a universal law governing the human family.

Its breach entails, as it has entailed, serious consequence for us. But the vast majority of men unwittingly follow the hereditary occupation of their fathers. Hinduism rendered a great service to mankind by the discovery of and conscious obedience to this law. If man's, as distinguished from lower animals, function is to know God, it follows that he must not devote the chief part of his life to making experiments in finding out what occupation will best suit him for earning his livelihood. On the contrary, he will recognize that it is best for him to follow his father's occupation, and devote his spare time and talent to qualifying himself for the task to which mankind is called.

Here then the difficulty suggested by my correspondent does not arise. For no one is precluded from rendering multitudinous acts of voluntary service and qualifying oneself for it. Thus Sjt. Nadkarni born of Brahmin parents and I born of Vaisya parents may consistently with the law of *varna* certainly serve as honorary national volunteers or as honorary nurses or honorary scavengers in times of need, though in obedience to that law he as a Brahmin would depend for his bread on the charity of his neighbours and I as a Vaisya would be earning my bread by selling drugs or groceries. Everyone is free to render any useful service so long as he does not claim reward for it.

In this conception of the law of varna no one is superior to any other. All occupations are equal and honourable in so far as they are not in conflict with morals', private or public. A scavenger has the same status as a Brahmin. Was it not Max Muller who said that it was in the Hinduism more than in any other religion that life was no more and no less than Duty?

There is no doubt that at some stage of its evolution Hinduism suffered corruption, and the canker of superiority and inferiority entered and vitiated it. But this notion of inequality seems to me to be wholly against the spirit of sacrifice which dominates everything in Hinduism. There is no room for arrogation of superiority by one class over another in a scheme of life based on *ahimsa* whose active form is undefiled love for all life.

Let it not be said against this law of *varna* that it makes life dull and robs it of all ambition. In my opinion that law of *varna* alone makes life livable by all and restores the only object worthy of it, namely, self-realization. Today we seem to think of and strive for material pursuits which are in their very nature transitory, and we do this almost to the exclusion of the one thing needful.

If I am told that the interpretation put by me upon *varna* is not supported by anything to be found in the *smritis* which are codified

Hindu conduct, my answer is that the codes of conduct based upon fundamental invariable maxims of life vary from time to time as we gain fresh experience and make fresh observations. It is possible to show many rules of the *smritis* which we no longer recognize as binding or even worthy of observance. Invariable maxims are few and common to all religions. The latter vary in their application. And no religion has exhausted the varieties of all possible applications. They must expand with the expansion of ideas and knowledge of new facts. Indeed I believe that the contents of words grow with the growth of human experience. The connotation of the words sacrifice, truth, non-violence, *varnashrama* etc., is infinitely richer today than it was during the known historic past. Applying this principle to the word *varna*, we need not be bound, it would be foolish and wrong to be bound, by the current interpretation, assuming that it is inconsistent with the requirements of the age with our notions of morals. To do otherwise will be suicide.

Varna considered in the manner above indicated has nothing in common with caste as we know it today, nor is prohibition as to inter- dining and intermarriage an essential part of the recognition of the law of *varna*. That these prohibitions were introduced for the conservation of *varnas* is possible. Restrictions against promiscuous marriage are necessary in any scheme of life based on self-restraint. Restraints on promiscuous dining arise either from sanitary considerations or differences in habits. But disregard of these restrictions formerly carried, or what is more, should now carry no social or legal punishment or forfeiture of one's varna.

Varnas were originally four. It was an intelligent and intelligible division. But the number is no part of the law of *varna*. A tailor, for instance, may not become a blacksmith although both may be and should be classed as Vaisyas.

The most forcible objection I heard raised in Tamilnadu was that, however good and innocuous varnas might appear under my interpretation, they must either be worked under a different name or destroyed altogether by reason of the evil odour that surrounds them. The objectors feared that my interpretation would be ignored and yet my authority would be freely quoted for supporting under cover of varna the hideous inequalities and tyrannies practised at the present day in Hinduism. They further observed that in the popular estimation caste and varna were mere synonymous terms and that the restraint of varna was nowhere practised, but the tyranny of caste was rampant everywhere. All these objections have no doubt much force in them. But they are objections such as can be advanced against many corrupted institutions that once were good. A reformer's business is to examine the institution itself and to set about reforming it if its abuses can be separated from it. Varna is not a mere institution made by man but it is a law discovered by him. It cannot therefore be set aside; its hidden meaning and potentialities should be explored and utilized for the good of society. We have seen that the evil is not in the law or the institution itself, but it lies in the doctrine of superiority and inferiority which are superadded to it.

The question too arises how the law is to be worked in these days when all the four varnas or sub-varnas break as under all the restrictions, seeking by all means lawful and otherwise to advance their material welfare, and when some arrogate superiority over others who in their turn are rightly challenging the claim. The law will work itself out even if we ignore it. But that will be the way of punishment. If we will escape destruction, we will submit to it. And seeing that we are just now engaged in applying to ourselves the sub-human rule of survival of the fittest, meaning the strongest (physically), it would be well to recognize ourselves as one Varna, viz., Sudras, even though some may be teaching and some may be soldiering and some others may be engaged in commercial pursuits. I remember in 1915 the Chairman at the Social Conference in Nellore suggesting that formerly all were Brahmins and that now too all should be recognized as such and that the other varnas should be abolished. It appeared to me then, as it appears to me now, as a weird suggestion. Itis the so-called superior that has to descend from his heights, if the reform is to be peaceful. Those who for ages have been trained to consider themselves as the lowest in the social scale cannot suddenly have the equipment of the so-called higher classes. They can therefore rise to power only by bloodshed, in other words by destroying society itself. In the scheme of reconstruction I have in view, no mention has been made of the untouchables, for I find no place for untouchability in the law of varna or otherwise in Hinduism. They in common with the rest will be absorbed in the Sudra. Out of these the other three varnas will gradually emerge purified and equal in status though differing in occupations. The *Brahmins* will be very few. Fewer still will be the soldier class who will not be the hirelings or the unrestrained rulers of today, but real protectors and trustees of the nation laying down their lives for its service. The fewest will be the Sudras for in a well-ordered society a minimum amount of labour will be taken from fellowmen. The most numerous will be the Vaisyas-a varna that would include all professions-the agriculturists, the traders, the artisans, etc. This scheme may sound Utopian. I, however, prefer to live in this Utopia of my imagination to try to live up to the unbridled licence of a society that I see tottering to its disruption. It is surely given to individuals to live their own Utopias even though they may not be able to see them accepted by society. Every reform has made its beginning with the individual, and that which had inherent vitality and the backing of a stout soul was accepted by the society in whose midst the reformer lived.

***

A correspondent writes:

"In your recent Madras speech you have re-stated your faith in the four *varnas*. But should the *varnas* be strictly hereditary? Some people think that you favour rigid adherence to the hereditary principle; others that you do not. From a perusal of your writings I am inclined to agree with the former. For instance, what else does your dictum, that the untouchables should be classed with Shudras' and that they should enjoy all the rights of non-Brahmins, indicate? Why this constant reiteration of the old arbitrary distinction between Brahmin and non-Brahmin as if the two belonged to biologically different species? If an untouchable can become a non-Brahmin, can he not also become a Brahmin in this very life? Again, if it is possible for an untouchable to become a Shudra, how is it impossible for a Shudra to become a Vaisya, for a Vaisya to become a Kshatriya or for a Kshatriya to become a Brahmin in this very life? Why do you hurl the Law of *Karma* in the face of those who believe it to be possible? Is there a better Brahmin than Sree Narayana Guru Swami, the Ezhava? I know no better Brahmin than Gandhiji, the Bania. I know also of hundreds of other 'non-Brahmins' who are better Brahmins (in the best sense of that term) than most birth-Brahmins.

If you did not favour strict application of the principle of heredity, you would not seek to prohibit intermarriages between people of the same race professing the same religion and following the same customs as are several members of the three *Dwija* castes. Nor would you so strenuously oppose inter-dining between, say, vegetarian Brahmins and vegetarian non-Brahmins.

Of course, heredity is a great law of life, but there are even greater laws controlling its mysterious processes. One of them is the law of variation in the phraseology of Evolutionary Biology. Heredity is the static and variation is the dynamic principle of the universe. The latter is that holds the key to what we call 'Progress' for want of a better name. No social system can ignore the law of heredity with impunity; neither can a social system ignore the law of variation except at its peril. The history of the caste system in India affords enough proof of this. It proves above all that the worst form in which the law of heredity can be applied in any social organization is to create a hereditary clergy to be the sole custodians of its intellectual and spiritual affairs and trustees in perpetuity of its religion.

Even Babu Bhagwan Das, than whom there is no more orthodox Brahmin and who has done some hard thinking on the subject of social reconstruction in India, conceded some years ago that the hereditary principle in *Varnashrama Dharma* must be considerably relaxed. It would be, indeed, strange if you of all men championed rigid adherence to it. As a great many people do not know what exactly you think of it all, I hope it will be possible for you to publish this letter with your reply in your esteemed journal."

I fancy that I have answered all the arguments advanced by the correspondent against *Varnashrama*. But evidently, readers have short memories or only those who are concerned for the moment read what is written for them. Thus, for instance, I have often shown the distinction between *Varnashrama* and untouchability. I have defended the one as a rational scientific fact and condemned the other as an excrescence, an unmitigated evil. It may be that my denseness sees a distinction where none exists. It may be too, that I see science where there is ignorance or superstition. But I do regard *Varnashrama* as a healthy division of work based on birth. The present ideas of caste are a perversion of the original. There is no question with me of superiority or inferiority. It is purely a question of duty. I have indeed stated that *varna* is based on birth. But I have also said that it is possible for a Shudra, for instance, to become a Vaisya. But in order to perform the duty of a Vaisya he does not need the label of a Vaisya. Swami Narayan Guru does not need to be called a Brahmin in order to enable him to be, what he is reported to be, a Sanskrit scholar. He who performs the duty of a Brahmin will easily become one in the next incarnation. But a translation from one *varna* to another in the present incarnation must result in a great deal of fraud. The natural consequence must be the obliteration (of) *varna*. I have seen no reason to justify its destruction. It may be a hindrance to material ambition. I must be excused from applying material considerations to an institution that is based on religious considerations.

Nor is the correspondent happy in his analogy. I have asked that a *Panchama* should be regarded as a Shudra because I hold that there is no warrant for belief in a fifth caste. A Panchama does the work of a Shudra and he is, therefore naturally classified as such when he ceases to be regarded as a *Panchama*. I do believe that this constant confusion between untouchability and *Varnashrama* and attack on the latter in the same breath as the former retards the progress of reform regarding untouchability.

It is now clear that the law of variation is left untouched by *Varnashrama*. Nay, it is provided for. Only, types do not vary in a few years or even in a few generations. There is no fundamental difference between a Brahmin and a Pariah, but he who runs may see that class considered, there is a marked and noticeable difference between Brahmins and Pariahs or for that matter all the four castes. What I would like my correspondent to join me in is a fight against an arrogant assumption of superiority whether it is assumed by Brahmins or others. It is the abuse, of *Varnashrama* that should be combated, not the thing itself.

CHAPTER-9

Brahmacharya

I am being inundated with letters on *brahmacharya* and means to its attachment. Let me repeat in different language what I have already said or written on previous occasions. *Brahmacharya* is not mere mechanical celibacy; it means complete control over all the senses and freedom from lust in thought, word and deed. As such it is the royal road to self- realization or attainment of *Brahman*.

The ideal *Brahmachari* has not to struggle with sensual desire or desire for procreation; it never troubles him at all. The whole world will be to him one vast family, he will centre all his ambition in relieving the misery of mankind and the desire for procreation will be to him as gall and wormwood. He who has realized the misery of mankind in all its magnitude will never be stirred by passion. He will instinctively know the fountain of strength in him, and he will ever persevere to keep it undefiled. His humble strength will command respect of the world, and he will wield an influence greater than that of the scepter monarch.

But I am told that this is an impossible ideal, that I do not take count of the natural attraction between man and woman. I refuse to believe that the sensual affinity referred to here can be at all regarded as natural; in that case the deluge would soon be over us. The natural affinity between man and woman is the attraction between brother and sister, mother and son, or father and daughter. It is that natural attraction that sustains the world. I should find it impossible to live, much less carry on my work, if I did not regard the whole of womankind as sisters, daughters or mothers. If I looked at them with lustful eyes, it would be the surest way to perdition.

Procreation is a natural phenomenon indeed, but within specific limits. A transgression of those limits imperils womankind, emasculates the race, induces disease, puts a premium on vice, and makes the world ungodly. A man in the grip of the sensual desire is a man without moorings. If such a one were to guide society, to flood it with his writings and men were to be swayed by them, where would society be? And yet we have the very thing happening today. Supposing a moth whirling round a light were to record the moments of its fleering joy and we were to imitate it, regarding it as an exemplar, where would we be? No, I must declare with all the power I can command that sensual attraction even between husband and wife is unnatural. Marriage is meant to cleanse the hearts of the couple of sordid passions and take them nearer to God. Lustless love between husband and wife is not impossible. Man is not a brute. He has risen to a higher state after countless births in brute creation. He is born to stand, not to walk on all fours or crawl. Bestiality is as far removed from manhood, as matter from spirit.

In conclusion, I shall summarize the means to its attainment. The first step is the realization of its necessity. The next is gradual control of the senses.

A *brahmachari* must needs to control his palate. He must eat to live, and not for enjoyment. He must see only clean things and close his eyes before anything un-clean. It is thus a sign of polite breeding to walk with one's eyes towards the ground and not wandering about from object to object. A *brahmachari will* likewise hear nothing obscene or unclean; smell no strong, stimulating things. The smell of clean earth is far sweeter than the fragrance of artificial scents and essences. Let the aspirant to *brahmacharya* also keep his hands and feet engaged in all the waking hours in healthful activity. Let him also fast occasionally.

The third step is to have clean companions-clean friends and clean books.

The last and not the least is prayer. Let him repeat Ramanama with all his heart regularly every day, and ask for divine grace.

None of these things are difficult for an average man or woman. They are simplicity itself. But their very simplicity is embarrassing. Where there is a will, the way is simple enough. Men have not will for it and hence vainly grope. The fact that the world rests on the observance, more or less, of *brahmacharya* or restraint, means that it is necessary and practicable.

Truth vs. Brahmacharya

A friend writes to Mahadev Desai:

> "You will remember that in an article on *brahmacharya* published in *Navajivan* sometime ago, translated in *Young India* by you, Gandhiji admitted that he still had bad dreams. The moment I read it I felt that such admissions could have no wholesome effect, and I came to know later that my fear was justified.
>
> During our sojourn in England, my friends and I kept our character unscathed in spite of temptations. We remained absolutely free from

wine, women and meat. But on reading Gandhiji's article one of the friends exclaimed to me in despair. 'If such is the case with Gandhiji even after his Herculean efforts, where are we? It is useless to attempt to observe *brahmacharya*. Gandhiji's confession has entirely changed my point of view. Take me to be lost from today.' Not without some hesitation, I tried to reason with him: 'If the way is so difficult for men like Gandhiji, it is much more so for us, and we should therefore redouble our effort'-the way Gandhiji or you would argue. But it was all in vain. A character that had been spotless so long was thus bespattered with mire. What would Gandhiji or you say if someone were to hold Gandhiji responsible for this fall?

As long as I had only one such instance in mind, I did not write to you. You would possibly have put me off by saying that it was an exceptional case. But there were more such instances and my fear has been more than justified.

I know that there are certain things which are quite easy for Gandhiji to achieve, and which are impossible for me. But by the grace of God, I can say that something which may be impossible for even Gandhiji may be possible for me. It is this consciousness, or pride that has saved me from a fall, though the admission above-mentioned has completely disturbed my sense of security.

Will you please invite Gandhi's attention to this fact, especially when he is just in the midst of his autobiography?

It is certainly brave to say the truth and the naked truth, but the world and the readers of *Navajivan* and *Young India* will misunderstand him. I fear that one man's meat may be another man's poison.

The complaint does not come to me as a surprise. When non-co-operation was in full swing, and when during the course of the struggle I confessed to an error of judgment a friend innocently wrote to me:

"Even if it was an error, you ought not to have confessed it. People ought to be encouraged to believe that there is at least one man who is infallible. You used to be looked upon as such. Your confession will now dishearten them."

This made me smile and also made me sad. I smiled at the correspondent's simpleness. But the very thought of encouraging people to believe a fallible man to be infallible was more than I could bear.

A knowledge of one as he is can always do good to the people, never any harm. I firmly believe that my prompt confessions of my errors have been all to the good for them. For me, at any rate, they have been a blessing:

And I may say the same thing of my admission about the bad dreams. It would do the world a lot of harm if I claimed to be a perfect *brahmachari* without being one. For it would sully *brahmacharya* and dim the lustre of truth. How dare I undervalue *brahmacharya* by false pretences? I can see today the means I suggest for the observance of *brahmacharya* are not adequate, are not found to be invariably efficacious, because I am not a perfect *brahmachari*. It would be an awful thing for the world to be allowed to believe that I was a perfect *brahmachari*, whilst I could not show the royal road to *brahmacharya*.

Why should it not be sufficient for the world to know that I am a genuine seeker, that I am wide awake, and that my striving is ceaseless and unbending? Why should not this knowledge be sufficient encouragement to others? It is wrong to deduce conclusions from false premises. It is wisest to draw them from things achieved. Why argue that because a man like me could not escape unclean thoughts, there is no hope for the rest? Why not rather argue that if a Gandhi, who was once given to lust, can today live as friend and brother to his wife and can look upon the fairest damsel as his sister or daughter, there is hope for the lowliest and the lost? If God was merciful to one who was so full of lust, certainly all the rest would have his mercy too.

The friends of the correspondent who were put back because of the knowledge of my imperfections had never gone forward at all. It was a false virtue that fell at the first blast. The truth and observance of *brahmacharya* and similar eternal principles do not depend on a person's imperfect as myself. They rest, on the sure foundations of the penance of the many that strove for them and lived them in their fullness. When I have the fitness to stand alongside those perfect beings, there will be much more determination and force in language than today. He whose thoughts do not wander and think evil, whose sleep knows no dreams and who can be wide awake even whilst asleep, is truly healthy. He does not need to take quinine. His incorruptible blood will have the inherent virtue of resisting all infections. It is for such a perfectly healthy state of body, mind and spirit that I am striving. This knows no defeat or failure. I invite the correspondent, his friends of little faith, and others to join me in that striving, and I wish that they may go forward even like the correspondent quicker than I. Let my example inspire those who are behind me with more confidence. All that I have achieved has been in spite of my weakness, in spite of my liability to passion-and because of my ceaseless striving and infinite faith in God's grace.

No one need therefore despair. My Mahatmaship is worthless. It is due to my outward activities, due to my politics which is the least part of me and is therefore evanescent. What is of abiding worth is my insistence on truth, non-violence and *brahmacharya* which is the real part of me. That permanent part of me however small, is not to be despised. It is my all. I prize even the failures and disillusionments which are but steps towards success.

Brahmacharya means not merely mechanical celibacy, but it means complete control over all the organs and senses enabling one to attain perfect freedom from all passion and hence from sin in thought, word and deed.

Importance of Tapas

There are instances of *tapas* (penance) at every step in Hindu mythology. Parvati desired to win Shankara and she took to *tapas*. Siva did something wrong and so he undertook *tapas*. Vishwamitra was the very incarnation of *tapas*. When Rama went into exile, Bharata plunged into yoga discipline, practised austere *tapas* and wore out his body.

God cannot test man in any other manner. If the soul is different from the body, it should remain blissful even when the body is tormented. Food is nourishment for the body, whereas knowledge and meditation are sustenance to the soul. Everyone has to realize this for himself as and when occasion arises.

If, however, the *tapas is* accompanied by faith, devotion and humility, then all that austerity becomes a futile exercise. It also becomes hypocrisy. A devotee of God who enjoys eating his meal is a thousand times better than such an ascetic.

I have not the strength today to narrate the story *of tapas* but I may state that I cannot possibly live without *tapas*. Once again I am destined to plunge into the stormy ocean. Please, God, know that I am humble and protect me.

CHAPTER-10

Five Great Yajnas

There can be many ways of interpreting *yajna*. For the Hindu householder, five *yajnas* are considered essential: the oven, the pestle, the quern, the pitcher and the spinning-wheel. The fewer there are o/ these the less substantial the household. A glance at them, however, will show that the important sacrifices are the first and the last and the middle three are their offshoots. The quern, the pitcher and the pestle presuppose the oven. The oven would not work at its best in the absence of the quern or the pestle in a home, but still it can pull on. But stop the spinning wheel and you are without a principal organ. You have paralysis. A man who does no *yajna* for his food and clothing has no right to either. There should be a custom that he who does not work at his stove must go without food, and he who does not reply, his spinning wheel must go naked. We have discarded the spinning-wheel without discarding clothes. He is a thief who wears clothes without doing any spinning, in the same way that he who consumes food without working for it is a thief. *Yajna* means an offering, a sacrifice of the self, which is what physical labour is. They who work at the oven and the wheel are engaged in an intelligent sacrifice. Even those who are not engaged in such beneficial physical effort have to take some exercise to digest their food.

It will perhaps be clear now what a sin we have committed in giving up the spinning-wheel. India was a happy country, healthy and bright, when in the past millions of its women used to engage themselves in this light but beneficial labour. Today, by giving it up, the country has become miserable, diseased and listless.

The oven, the spinning-wheel, etc., are each of them a veritable grace of the home. If millions of Indian homes are in ruins today, it is because we gave up the spinning-wheel. Let no one suppose that this is an exaggeration. It is possible the reader's own home is not in that condition. But then a shortage of water does not mean that no one can get any water. It means everyone has less than before, many have very little, while some have none at all. Similarly, many families may be able to carry on without the spinning-wheel, but some at least have been completely ruined. Look at Orissa and Champaran. A number of villages there are ruined. What else would happen to a country whose people, 150 years ago, had some work or other all the year round, but 80 per cent of who today are unemployed for four months in the year?

Work alone is real wealth; metal is a mere token for it. When 80 percent of people are unemployed for four months, their earning capacity is reduced by one-third. Despite the capacity and willingness to earn Rs. 3, Indians have for years been working to earn no more than Rs. 2. They cannot find work for more than that. How could such a country not help being poor? The only remedy for such a state of affairs is a vow to wear *khadi* made from yarn spun with our own hands. Then we shall take to the spinning-wheel, willy-nilly, and realize finally that we had made a mistake in giving it up. But, in the meantime, we ought to undertake a determined effort to popularize it. We shall never be eager to introduce the spinning-wheel, nor after introducing it, shall we be keen to ply it, so long as we continue to be as fond of foreign cloth as we are. A vow to discard foreign cloth will compel us to use the spinning-wheel. Thus the spinning-wheel and boycott of foreign cloth are closely inter-related. We hardly care for a thing that is not a necessity. It is, therefore, our sacred duty to see that the spinning-wheel becomes a necessity. There is no other way of eradicating India's poverty. For the mistake of giving up so invaluable a thing, there can be no adequate atonement. A small sacrifice may be enough if we make it on our own. If we are to do things under compulsion, who can say what they will be?

CHAPTER-11

Untouchability

A friend has asked some questions about untouchability which I believe I ought to answer as best as I may and which, therefore, I give below:

In my opinion, untouchability in the form in which we practice it today is not and ought not to be, an essential part of Hinduism. There is sheer ignorance and cruelty behind it. I look upon it as an excrescence on Hinduism. It. does not protect religion, but suffocates it. Its practice on certain occasions, as during the days following the death of a near relation, is in a different class. One may follow it to the extent one wants to. It is not followed with equal rigidity by all communities. The practice of untouchability in this form should bc treated as a matter of hygiene. To a greater or less extent, some such regulations are found all over the world. But treating Antyajas as untouchables is a cruel form of a boycott. Whatever justification there may have been for the practice when it started, there is none now. Like tuberculosis, therefore, it is eating into the vitals of Hinduism.

Just as the many dilapidated and useless parts of a building, if not pulled down, weaken the rest of the building, so the outer wall of untouchability weakens, instead of protecting, the inner wall of restrictions in regard to eating in company and marrying outside one's circle. It is true that, in the same way as we look upon untouchability as an evil, there are some who regard these restrictions also as an evil and attack them as such. There is, however, some reasonable principle behind them. It would ordinarily be improper for a conscientious vegetarian to eat at a non-vegetarian's place. But I see no *dharma* in treating as untouchables those who do not follow the rules that we do. No one practices such a *dharma*. Anyone who wants to practice it would have to treat everyone else in the world as an untouchable.

The movement for the eradication of untouchability has no connection with the problem of caste. However, according to the rule that one important reform leads to another, reformers have turned their eyes to the problem of caste-division too. I desire the disappearance or sub-castes, and in fact they are disappearing. I do not, however, see the same evil in them as I see in the practice of untouchability. These subdivisions are a source of inconvenience. They obstruct social inter-course in some ways. But their abolition is a reform which can wait. The eradication of untouchability can wait and it is therefore, very necessary to keep the two apart and understand the distinction between then.

I find no harm in accepting clean water from a pot filled in a clean manner by a clean Antyaja. Ordinarily, members of other communities accept water served by Kunabis or Ghatis; that rule should also apply to Antyajas. That is, in dealing with them the same rule should be followed which the so-called upper castes generally follow in their intercourse with the other castes. In the South, where every non-Brahmin is an untouchable in the eyes of a Brahmin, the practice is an excrescence even on an excrescence. I have come across no one who would defend it, and the practice is gradually disappearing.

It is not true that Antyaja children must necessarily be dirty. I have seen many Antyaja children who were cleaner than other children. The only rule can be this; a child which does not pass a certain test of cleanliness ought not to be admitted to the school, or, all children who are dirty should be put in a separate division meant for them and should be given special instruction in cleanliness. To assume that Antyaja children must necessarily be dirty and refuse admission to a child even if he is clean, is to treat Antyajas in the same way in which Indians are treated in the Colonies. There, the very fact of having born an Indian is a crime. Generally speaking, the practical thing to do in the present circumstances is to start a large number of schools, especially for Antyaja children. However much we try, all Antyaja children will not be brought for enrolment in the general primary schools. Admission to general schools, therefore, should be open to such of them as observe the rule of cleanliness, but there should also be separate primary schools for them for their special encouragement.

Untouchability and Unapproachability

The accumulated burden of Hindus' sins is big enough. We have used *Shastras*, which teach selflessness, as instruments of selfishness. By casting aside the immutable principles enunciated in the *Shastras* and treating as of permanent application verses which prescribed rules of conduct of temporary utility, we have elevated wickedness to the place of *dharma. My* conscience tells me even more emphatically every day that one such wickedness is the practice of untouchability. As if the sin of untouchability was not enough, we started another sinful practice, that of unapproachability, to add to the burden. In the South, that is, in Madras Presidency, the people are familiar with this sinful practice. But with a view to serving these people kept at a distance and atoning for their own sins, Hindu members of the Congress in Travancore have started *satyagraha*. Travancore is a Hindu State. There this practice of forcibly keeping people at a distance exists in cruel form. Many Gujaratis may not be even aware of the meaning of *doorata*. The word is not found in the dictionary, how can it ever be found in the *Shastras? Doorata* means the untouchables keeping at a certain distance from other Hindus. Owing to the belief that the other Hindus, and mainly Brahmins, are polluted even by the shadow cast by these untouchables, the latter are obliged to walk at some yards distance from the Brahmins and other Hindus. When passing along the same road, if they fail to do so, abuses and even blows are showered on them. There are some streets in Travancore which these poor brethren are forbidden even to enter. Pained by this unbearable evil, Hindu members of the Congress have started *satyagraha*, as I mentioned above. In order to establish his right to walk along a particular street, an untouchable Hindu takes with him another Hindu and enters that street. Three untouchables offer this kind of *satyagraha* every day and court arrest. Three of them, arrested in this way, are serving a six-month term of imprisonment. There is not the slightest doubt that, if this *satyagraha* continues peacefully and steadily, people will win.

The Hindus working to eradicate the evils of untouchability in North India have gone much further than this with the help and under the leadership of Bharat Bhushan Malviya: the Antyajas draw water from wells used by other Hindus. The notion of being defiled by their touch seems to have died out in many places. Now the classes regarded as untouchables are able to make use of common wells. The Secretary of the Dohad Taluka Congress Committee reports to this effect. He writes to say that the Hindus did not permit the Antyajas to draw water from a well belonging to the local board. A weaver who had passed the vernacular final examination made bold to use the well and persuaded other members of his community to follow him. They agreed and went to fetch water from that well. Other Hindus attempted to stop them from doing so, but the police sub-inspector refused to help them and explained to them that, when a movement was going on in the country against such restrictions, they should not try to stop the Antyajas. That calmed the caste Hindus. This was a happy conclusion. The incident, however, shows that, even in Gujarat, the Antyajas are still prevented from drawing water from public wells. I congratulate the Hindus of Dohad, but at the same time suggest to the Dohad Congress committee members that they should visit the Antyaja locality and instruct the residents in sanitation and persuade them to keep their pitchers, etc., clean. If such an effort to reform them is not undertaken simultaneously it is likely that, while things are just beginning to change for the better, opposition to Antyajas drawing water from public wells may be renewed. I have heard of such a development at many places in the north.

Varnashrama and Untouchability

A correspondent writes:

> "With reference to your comments on my letter on *Varnashrama* published in *Young India* of the 23rd April 1925, I fully appreciate the distinction between *Varnashrama* and untouchability and agree that there is no sanction whatsoever for the latter in Hinduism. But is it not clear that, if the principle of 'division of work based on birth' which you approve continues to be the basis of our social organization, the untouchable will be always with us? What is more reasonable than to suppose that in that case those members of society who hereditarily perform such social duties as scavenging, corpse-bearing and grave-digging will continue to be looked upon as too unclean to be touched by the rest of the community? In all other countries, scavengers, cobblers, barbers, washermen, grave-diggers, undertakers, etc, are not considered untouchable either as individuals or as a class for the simple reason that in those countries these occupations are not hereditary and any member of any of the classes can at any time become a soldier, trader, teacher, lawyer, politician or priest. It seems to me, therefore, that the root of the *evil* of the untouchability so peculiar to our country lies in our peculiar social system exclusively based on the principle of heredity. And it also seems to me that so long as we adhere to that principle we cannot hope to get rid of untouchability. It is just conceivable that, under the influence of mighty reformers like Ramanuja or under the stress of a strong political passion, its virulence may abate from time to time but the evil cannot be wholly eliminated. I am afraid that every attempt to end untouchability without ending the caste idea will prove as futile as attempting to cut off a tree at its top."

The letter is very plausible and, unless the reformer takes care, the danger which the correspondent fears may become a stem reality. There is, however, a clear confusion of thought in the argument. Does untouchability in the case of a cobbler or scavenger attach to birth or to occupation? If it attaches to birth, it is hideous and must be rooted out; if it attaches to occupation, it may be sanitary rule of great importance. It is of universal application. A collier, whilst he is engaged in his work, is practically an untouchable. He himself refuses to shake the hand extended to him and says, "I am too dirty." But his work finished, he takes his bath, changes his dress, and very properly mixes with die highest in the land. Immediately, therefore, we remove the taint of birth, i.e., the ideas of superiority and inferiority attaching to birth, we purify *Varnashrama*. The scavenger's children may remain scavengers without being or feeling degraded and they will be no more considered untouchables than Brahmins. The fault does not, therefore, lie in recognizing the law of heredity and transmission of qualities from generation to generation, but it lies with the faulty conception of inequality

Varnashrama, in my opinion, was not conceived in any narrow spirit. On the contrary, it gave the labourer, the Sudra, the same status as the thinker, the Brahmin. It provided for the accentuation of merit and elimination of demerit, and it transferred human ambition from the general worldly sphere to the permanent and the spiritual. The aim of the Brahmin and the Sudra was *common-moksha*, or self-realization-not realization of fame, riches and power. Later on, this lofty conception of *Varnashrama* became degraded and came to be identified with mere empty ceremonial and assumption of superiority by some and imposition of degradation upon others. This admission is not a degradation of the weakness of *Varnashrarma*, but of human nature which, if it has a tendency under certain circumstances to rise to the highest point, it has also a tendency under certain other circumstances to go down to the lowest. What the reformer seeks to do is to end the curse of untouchability and to restore *Varnashrama* to its proper place. Whether *Varnashrama* thus transmitted will survive the reform or not remains to be seen. It will surely depend upon the new Brahmin that is imperceptibly coming into being, namely, those who are dedicating themselves, body, soul and mind, to service of Hinduism and the country. If they have nothing of worldly ambition, it will be well with Hinduism, if they have, Hinduism, like any other *ism*, coming into the hand of ambitious men will perish. But I have an immutable faith in the capacity of Hinduism to purge itself of all impurities from time to time. I do not think that capacity is now exhausted.

Sometime during the last month two Japanese friends came to me, engaged me in a pleasant conversation and left with me the following document:

"The great spirits of India once came to Japan through China".

They made great influences upon the whole of the souls of Japanese. The influences still have upon us Japanese and will have ever, so Japanese pay great special respects to India.

Now I am here in India-so much respected country by our people-I feel quite happy.

Even in the present time, at our own age, there came out a greatest man who is wholly self-sacrificed and absolutely honest to the justice and truth.

It should be great happiness to me if I should be allowed to be present before him and should be permitted to be given some influences from him directly.

We know him only through books and newspapers. There may be some misunderstandings on us to know about him.

Let me have honour to be given some of his opinions upon our thoughts.

Men are born naked. But to them two hands are given.

We think God has given paradise upon men, but he has not given it directly upon men. He has given it indirectly upon them by giving two hands-the power to create any and everything-to make paradise itself in the present world, so I think it is the duty of man to make use their hands best. For instance, they must make clothes with many variety and beauty to fit to several climates and different occasions. And in some occasions they must be clothed more beautiful than wild beasts and fowls, more beautiful than the skin of tigers or peacocks. Because to be beautiful is one essential thing in paradise with to be good and to be truth.

To make railroads, steamers, and many different machines is our duty and we must utilize them with utmost efficiency, so yarn system, make pardon to say, I think, is not the final end of our purposes to attain, only one of means to teach people to be thrift, frugality, sound minded and such as to give other many good influences upon them, and make utilize plenty of time in country lives where many hands are left idle."

I have purposely refrained from making any corrections, for its quaintness would then be gone. I wish I had read this document before seeing these friends, in which case I would have told them that it was my realization of the fact that God has given us two hands that made me think of asking millions of the inhabitants of this land not to allow them to remain idle for a single minute, but to make the best use possible of them so as to be able, by their use during leisure hours, to clothe the whole of India. I would also have asked my visitors to help us to realize our destiny by inducing Japan not to inflict her cloth upon us, but to engage only in such commerce with us as would be mutually beneficial. Finally, I would have told them that I had no quarrel with railroads, steamers and many different machines as such, but that I protested against the abuse that was at present being made of them, either for exploiting many nations of the earth or for destroying them.

Vaishnavas and Antyajas

I drew attention to the virtues of the true *Vaishnava* which Narasinh Mehta, the great *Vaishnava*, has sung of in his poem, and I expressed my pain at the comments on my talk with Maharajshri.

I saw in them, not an attempt to determine the meaning of *dharma*, but only *duragraha* and attacks on mc. May it not be said that I, too, am guilty of *dura*-graha and attack others? Certainly, it may. It will be for the reader to judge whether this is true or not. At the very beginning of our talk, Maharajshri told me that, in the interpretation of *shastras*, reason had no scope. That itself pained me. In my view, that which reason cannot understand and which the heart does not accept can be no *shastra*, and I think that anyone who wants to follow *dharma* in its purity cannot but admit this principle. If we do not do this, we shall run the risk of violating our *dharma*. I have heard the 'Gita' being interpreted to the effect that, if any of our relations are wicked, we may use force to reduce them to submission; indeed, that it is our *dharma* to do so. Because Rama killed Ravana, is it *dharma* to kill a person whom we regard as Ravana? The *Manusmriti* permits the eating of meat; is a *Vaishnava* free, therefore, to eat meat? I have had it from the lips of *shastris* and men claiming to be *sannyasis* that, when ill, one may take even beef. Where would I have been if, accepting all these interpretations of *shastras*, I had gone about destroying my relatives, had advised the killing of the British and eaten beef in my illness? On such occasions, I was saved because I accepted only that as *dharma* which my reason and my heart accepted as such, and I advise everyone to do the same.

For this reason, holy men of *tapashcharya* have told us that those who study the Vedas but do not follow *dharma* in conduct are mere pedants; that they neither swim across themselves, nor help others to do so. So it is that I am never impressed by those who have the Vedas on their lips or have got the commentaries by heart and, instead of marvelling at their learning cherish my little knowledge as of greater value.

These being my views, I was pained when Maharajshri enunciated the principle for determining the meaning of *shastra*, but I was also pleased by his frankness. Though he held, thus, that the *shastras* were against me, his decision finally was that it would not be justice to exclude Antyajas from schools which were open to Muslims, Parsis, Christians, Jews and others. *Vaishnavas*, who give money for innumerable worldly activities and spend it even in gambling and similar things, could not take cover behind objections on religious grounds and refuse donations to national schools which admit Antyajas along with others. If they do not wish to send their children to schools attended by Antyajas, they should be under no pressure to do so. This was the pragmatic decision which Maharajshri gave.

However, the arguments of the *shastris* who surrounded Maharajshri made my heart sink. I saw no frankness in them, but only an obstinate clinging to their views. Shastri Vasantram has given us a sample of this in Gujarati.

I wish respectfully to tell him and the editor of Gujarati that a public worker's duty is not to follow the popular current but should its direction be wrong, to lead it in the right direction.

I do not know the *shastras*, have no experience, am obstinate-by asserting all this I cannot be disqualified from being a *Vaishnava*. So long as I hold that the test of being a *Vaishnava* lies in moral conduct and not in debating or the gift of clever speech or in determining the meaning of the *shastras, I* do not wish to give up my claim (of being a *Vaishnava*).

To say that looking upon the practice of untouchability as sin is a Western idea is to make out a sin to be a virtue. Akha Bhagat had no Western education but it was he who said in a poem, "Like a superfluous limb is this notion of defilement by touch". It is sheer fanaticism, and will lead to the degradation of *dharma*, to look upon efforts at eradicating our evils as deriving their inspiration from other religions and to cling on those evils.

It has been argued that the practice of untouchability implies no contempt; the British put forward a similar argument in regard to their attitude to us. If they keep us away, call us "natives", they mean no contempt (they say). If they force us to occupy separate compartments in trains, it is entirely for "convenience of hygiene" and there is no ill will in the procedure-such is their claim. I have seen *Vaishnavas* abusing and beating up Antyajas who happened to touch them unintentionally. It is sheer hypocrisy, or sin rather, to describe such conduct as *dharma*. There is arrogance in ordering Antyajas to turn their faces to the wall when a Brahmin is out in the street. It is baseless to offer them the remains on our plates or things which have become rotten. Such conduct has its source in the practice of untouchability.

I simply do not understand the contention that bathing and putting on clean clothes will not cleanse an Antyaja. Is it that an Antyaja carries filth in his heart, or that he was not born a human being? Are Antyajas lower even than animals?

I have seen a number of Antyajas who were of an open frank heart, were upright, and were men of knowledge and lovers of God. I look upon such Antyajas as worthy of all reverence.

I can understand the refusal to touch an Antyaja who is dirty or who has not bathed after carrying night-soil. But it is the very limit of *adharma* to refuse to touch Antyajas however clean. I have seen many who were not Antyajas but were extremely dirty. There are many Christians among those who carry night-soil. It is part of a physician's duty to help remove stools. We do not consider contact with these as sinful. But we despise our physicians who hold no degrees, committing a sin thereby and bringing a bad name to the *Vaishnava dharma*.

It seems, rather, that Shastri Vasantram and the editor of Gujarati have identified the practice of untouchability with *varnashrama*. In my humble opinion, the latter is *dharma*, unalterable, universal and in harmony with Nature, as also a social arrangement; it is a pure outward form of Hinduism.

The practice of untouchability is a blot on Hinduism; it was probably introduced as a temporary expedient, during the period of decline. It is based on no principle of universal application and has no support in the *shastras*. The verses which are cited in justification of it are interpolations; or, at any rate, there are differences of opinion about their meaning. There are no statements by *Vaishnavas* describing the practice of untouchability to be a part of *dharma*. It is disappearing day by day. It is not observed in trains, Government schools, centers of pilgrimage and courts. In mills and other big factories, people touch Antyajas with the utmost freedom. My request to *Vaishnavas* is that this contact with the Antyajas which in any case they tolerate, though looking upon it as sinful, they should accept deliberately and as an act of virtue. The 'Gita' says the same thing: "To the man who looks on all with an equal eye, a Brahmin, a dog and Antyaja-all are the same." 'Narsainyo' says in his poem that a Vaishnava should have the same eye for all. *Vaishnavas* cannot claim that they can maintain this attitude to Antyajas though looking upon them as people, with whom all contact is forbidden.

More about Antyajas

I feel sorry that *Navajivan* has had to join the present controversy about Antyajas. Since, however, the issue ha$ a bearing on the success of non-co-operation; I hope the readers of *Navajivan* will forgive me for taking up its space. It is *Navajivan's* duty to place before the people the naked truth as the workers who run the journal see it.

The path of non-cooperation is both easy and difficult. It is easy for those who understand it. For the others, it is difficult; for, not understanding it, they get confused again and again.

Problems do not get solved by our trying to put them out of sight. The path of non-cooperation will be easier if we solve a problem the moment it arises. Unless we co-operate among ourselves, we shall not acquire the strength to employ non-cooperation against the Government We shall not succeed if we look upon six crores of Antyajas as untouchable and despise them. An Empire which has set the Hindus and the Muslims against each other will not hesitate to create enmity between the Antyajas and the rest of the Hindus.

In forming our judgments, it is desirable that we are not led away by wrong information. The resolution that Antyajas will be admitted to schools recognized by the Vidyapith is not a new rule; it merely asserts what is implied in the constitution of the Vidyapith. The interpretation which it contains has not been inspired by Mr Andrews; he asked a question and the resolution was a reply to his question. The reply would have been the same if anyone else had asked the question.

I have said earlier that the resolution was not mine or that of any individual; it was of the Vidyapith's senate as a whole.

The resolution was adopted not as a measure of expediency but as an imperative moral obligation.

Its adoption is not the work of the new wind from the West but only means accepting what Hinduism says." I myself would not sacrifice *dharma* for the sake of *swaraj*. I have been fighting for *swaraj* because I think of it as an essential aspect of *dharma*.

I would be ready even to sacrifice the country for the sake of *dharma*; such is the ideal which inspires me. My patriotism is subject to my concern for *dharma* and, therefore, if the interest of the country conflicts with that of *dharma*, I would be ready to sacrifice the former. I look upon it as *adharma to* treat Antyajas as untouchables, and I have not the slightest wish to advance the interests of the country through *adharma*. I am convinced that we shall get *swaraj* only when there is religious awakening in the country. This awakening seems to be near at hand and that is the reason why I believe it possible to win *Swaraj* within one year. What I have said so far will have made it clear that, if I have been striving hard to eradicate the practice of untouchability, it is because I look upon it as *adharma*.

I am sure Hinduism does not at all teach that there can be any person who is born an untouchable and must die an untouchable. To describe such *adharma* as *dharma* is to be guilty of a further violation of *dharma*. *I* have been entreating the Hindus of Gujarat to give up, on rational grounds, the idea of untouchability which in any case is not followed in practice. If the idea had been right from the point of view of *dharma* and had disappeared in practice at the present time, I would have wished to revive it in the Vidyapith. But it is because I believe that the idea is contrary to *dharma* that I have welcomed the resolution of the Vidyapith and request all Gujaratis to do the same.

I realize that it is difficult to overcome old prejudices. Those who see the practice of untouchability in the light of a prejudice and cannot get rid of it all at once have my sympathy. But I merely pity those who keep it alive because they think it is *dharma*.

It is dangerous to give credence to everything which may be said in the name of Hinduism or the *shastras*. I, therefore, request the Gujarati Hindus not be misled by the resolution passed (at the meeting held) under the presidentship of the Shankaracharya.

It is very necessary, however, that in all our discussion we remain peaceful. This is especially true of the non-cooperator. I read in one of the articles of Shastri Vasantram that someone has held out a threat to him. We shall not succeed in solving religious issues or coming to the right decisions in any other matter by resorting to violence. We can decide between right and wrong only by reasoning with one another in a respectful manner. All moral problems will be resolved by each one of us acting on his ideas. The truth will emerge when we try to do so. Trying to throw dust-up at the sky we only fill our own eyes with it. Where is the need to argue this? Those who enjoy throwing dust will certainly throw it and learn, from experience, what is right and what is not. The effort to win swaraj while clinging to the sin of untouchability, a load of dirt, is like the attempt to throw dust-up at the sky

❍

CHAPTER-12

Two Speeches on Untouchability

I am very glad to see present here such a large number of people belonging to non-Antyaja communities.

I have been studying the conditions of the Antyaja communities for many years now. On this matter, I differ from our great reformers. I do not follow the same method of work as they do. I have been thinking over their method of work ever since my return to India, but I have not felt the work I have been doing is inadequate or that the work of others is better than mine. It is possible, of course that my work is inadequate, but my faith is that it is not.

My method of work is this. The practice of untouchability is a sin and should be eradicated. I look upon it as my duty to eradicate this sin; it is, however, to be eradicated on the initiative of the other Hindus, not the Antyajas. The practice of untouchability is an excrescence on Hinduism. I said once in Madras that I saw terrible Satanism in our Empire and that, if I could not mend it, I wanted to end it; likewise, I believe that the practice of untouchability is a great Satanism in Hinduism.

The late Mr Gokhale, on being acquainted with all the facts about our position in South Africa, asked why it should surprise us that our condition was so miserable. Just as we look upon the Antyajas as untouchables, so the Europeans look upon all of us, Hindus and Muslims, as untouchables. We may not reside in their midst, nor enjoy the rights which they do. The whites of South Africa have reduced Indians to the same miserable plight to which we Hindus have reduced the Antyajas. In the Colonies of the Empire, outside India the conduct of the whites (towards Indians) is exactly like that of the Hindus towards the Antyajas. It was this which prompted Shri Gokhale to say that we were tasting the fruit of the Satanism practised by Hindu society, that it had committed a great sin, had been guilty of extreme Satanism, and that this was the reason for our wretched plight in South Africa. I immediately agreed. What he said was perfectly right. My subsequent experience has confirmed it.

I am a Hindu myself and I claim to be an orthodox one. It is my further claim that I am a *sanatani* Hindu. At present, I am engaged in a great dispute with the Hindus in Gujarat. They, especially the *Vaishnavas*, reject my claim to be called a *sanatani* Hindu, but I cling to it and assert that I am one. This is one great evil in Hindu society. There are many others, but those you may eradicate, if not today after a thousand years and the delay may be forgiven. This practice, however, of regarding the Antyajas as untouchables is intolerable to me. I cannot endure it. The Hindus owe it as a duty to make a determined effort to purify Hinduism and eradicate this practice of untouchability. I have said to the Hindus, and say it again today, that till Hindu society is purged of this sin, *swaraj* is an impossibility. If you trust my words, I tell you that I am more pained by this evil being a part of the Hindu religion than the Antyajas are by them being treated as untouchables. While the practice remains in Hindu society, I feel ashamed and feel unhappy even to call myself a Hindu. The speakers, who preceded me and spoke to you in Marathi, made a kind of attack (on me). I would be (they said) worthy of the tide (Mahatma) which the country has conferred on me but which I have not accepted- only when Hinduism was purged of the evil of untouchability. When I am pouring out my heart, please do not interrupt me with applause. I ask you, tell me if you can; is there any method of work by following which one individual may end a very old practice? If anyone could show me such a way, I would end the thing today. But it is a difficult task to get Hindu society to admit its error and correct it.

I put into practice what I say. I have had to suffer much in trying to carry my wife with me in what I have been doing. By referring to my ordeals I want to show to you, Antyajas and Hindus, that this is a task full of great difficulties. I don't wish to suggest that we should on that account give it up. Only we should take thought about the method of work. This is my reason for not approving of your resolutions.

You want to pass a resolution to the effect that the Antyajas should be free to enter all the temples. How is this possible? So it is in vain that you ask that every Hindu should be-free to enter a temple right now. It is impossible to get society to accept this. It is not prepared for this yet. I know from experience that there are many temples which some other communities besides the Antyajas are also forbidden to enter. Some of the temples in Madras are not open even to me. I don't feel unhappy about this. I am not even prepared to say that this betrays the Hindus' narrow outlook or that it is a wrong they are committing. May be it is, but we should consider the line of thinking behind it. If their action is inspired by considerations of discipline, I would not say that everyone should be free to go into any temple. There are a variety of sects in India and I do not want to see them wiped out. Hindu society has not fallen because of sects or on account of *Varnashrama*. It has fallen because we have forgotten the beauty and the discipline which lie behind *Varnashrama* You should understand that *Varnashrama-dharma* has nothing to do with the practice of untouchability. To say that the former is evil, that it is a sin, is to apply Western standards, and I do not accept them. It is by accepting them that India has fallen. I do not want to have the blessings and the goodwill of the Antyajas for what I have not done and, therefore, I wish to make it plain to you on this occasion that I have associated myself with these proceedings most reluctantly. For I am with the Antyajas and the reformers in wanting to eradicate the evil of untouchability, but I do not go along with them in the other things which you and they want to be done. I cannot tell a Hindu-for I do not believe in it-which he may freely eat and drink in the company of any other Hindus or that all Hindus should freely inter-marry. This is not necessary. A man who refrains from these things, I say, may be a man of self-control or he may even be a man of licence. I believe that is with a view to self-control that people refrain from them.

I myself eat and drink in the company of Antyajas. I have adopted the daughter of an Antyaja family and she is dearer to me than my very life. I should not however, tell Hindu society that it might abandon self-control. I believe the society has a place even for one like me. It has a place for anyone who lives as I do, without being a *sannyasi* .Just as I would eat some thing offered by a Muslim, if it was otherwise acceptable, so I would accept anything offered by an Antyaja. But I should not like to compel other Hindus to do likewise, for it would mean their casting off self-control, the self-control which protects Hindu society. To abolish *Varnashrama* or the restrictions about eating and drinking and to eradicate the evil of untouchability-these two are not quite the same thing. One is Satanism, the other means self-control. I am a student and I have been studying this matter. If, therefore, I ever feel that I have been mistaken, I will forthwith admit my error; at the moment, however, I am ready to declare that I see nothing but hypocrisy, nothing but Satanism, in those who have been defending the practice of untouchability. It is Satanism which they are defending.

I have explained my limitations and the task to which I have addressed myself, as also my method of work. I do not believe that by working among the Antyajas and educating them, the reformers will succeed in eradicating the practice of untouchability. I know quite a few people who speak much on plat-forms but hang back when the occasion may require them to touch (an Antyaja). This method is not mine and I want to tell you that it is not the way to bring about reforms. On the other hand, those who argue that they will change their practice when Hindu society has corrected its error also weary me with their talk. I have been telling the Antyajas that I for one would most certainly offer non-cooperation against a man of this kind. I may tell all those other than Antyajas present here that, should all our efforts to eradicate this evil fail, it may even be that, alone, I shall offer non-cooperation against this sin of society-against Hindu society. I don't think it is so difficult to end the Satanism of the Empire. That Satanism is of a worldly nature. The Satanism of untouchability has taken on the colour of religion. Hindus are convinced that it is a sin to touch the Antyajas. It is a difficult task to make them see reason. We are so much in the grip of lethargy and inertia, so deeply sunk in misery that we can't even think. Our religious heads, too, are so deeply sunk in ignorance that it is impossible to explain things to them. Eradicating the evil of untouchability means, in fact, persuading Hindu society of its need. It will be impossible for the Antyajas to destroy the crores of Hindus and end the evil of untouchability. If the practice is enjoined in the Vedas or the *Manusmriti*, they ought to be replaced. But where are the men who will write new scriptures? I am a man of the world and lay no claim to being a religious leader. With many shortcomings myself, how can I lay down a moral and ethical code for the Hindus? I may only persuade them to do what I want by making myself worthy of their compassion.

The task is full of difficulties. However, if our reformers only realize that to seek to eradicate this evil by destroying Hindu society is a futile attempt, they will be convinced that they will achieve their purpose only by being patient. I tell you, my Antyaja friends, you are as much Hindus as I am, as much entitled to the privileges of Hinduism as I am. If you understand it properly, you have in your own hands the weapons you need, much as we have in our own hands the weapons we need to see an end of the empire. Just as begging will not avail us for this purpose, so also the means of ending the practice of untouchability is in the hands of Antyajas themselves.

If they ask me to teach them non-cooperation, I am ready to start this very evening. Non-cooperation is a process of self-purification. India is different from other lands and, therefore, we do not seek to get what we want by making things hot for the British. What then, is the way to purify ourselves? Hindus say that the Antyajas drink, that they eat anything and everything, that they do not observe rules of personal cleanliness, that they kill cows. I do not believe that all this is true. No one who claims to be a Hindu can eat beef. If the Antyajas want to employ non-cooperation, they should give up drinking and eating beef or, at any rate, killing cows. I do not ask the tanners to give up their work. Englishmen do this work but we don't mind saluting them. These days even Brahmins do it. I see no uncleanliness in doing sanitary work. I have myself done that work for a long time, and I like doing it. My mother taught me that it is holy work. Though it means handling unclean things, the work itself is holy. Anyone who does it and looks upon it as holy work will go to heaven. You can remain in the Hindu fold without giving it up. If anyone offers you leftover food or cooked food, you should refuse to accept it and ask him to give you grains instead. Be clean in your habits. When you have finished your work of cleaning latrines, change your dress. Though doing this work, you should observe as much cleanliness as my mother did. You will ask me how you are to get clothes into which you may change; you should, in that case, tell the Hindus that you will not work unless you get Rs. 15 or 20 or 30, whatever you think you need, you can tell them that you perform an essential service for society, in the same way, that carpenters and blacksmiths do. Make yourselves fearless. I know the Antyajas of Gujarat, know their nature, I teach them this same thing, that they should end the evil of untouchability by their own strength, that they should live as thorough-going Hindus so that other Hindus may honour them instead of despising them.

I want to get the thing done through you or through Hindu society itself. I ask you to make yourselves fit for the rights which you demand. By saying so, I do not wish to suggest that you are not already fit. When

I ask the country to be fit for *swaraj*, I do not imply that it is unfit. I only ask it to be fitter than it is. I tell the Antyajas, likewise, that they have a right to be free, to be the equal of any other Hindu; I ask them, however, to do *tapashcharya* and be fitter for these things.

Speaking of *tapashcharya*, *I* should like to tell you of two incidents in my life. After I had started the Satyagraha Ashram in Ahmedabad, I admitted to it an Antyaja friend, named Dudhabhai, and his wife. How did our Hindus behave at the time? Dudhabhai's wife was not allowed to draw water from the well which we had been using. I told them that, in that case, I, too, would not avail myself of that well. I had a share in the use of that well. But I let it go. How did Dudhabhai behave? He remained perfectly calm, bearing the abuse in silence. With this *tapashcharya*, the difficulty was overcome in three days, the people having realized that Dudhabhai too was free to draw water from that well. This same Dudhabhai's daughter, Laxmi, lives in my house, moving like (Goddess)

Lakshmi indeed. If all of you learnt to do the *tapashcharya* which Dudhabhai did, your suffering would be over this very day.

And now I address myself to Hindus other than Antyajas and tell them that they should be brave and get rid of this sin of theirs. I believe that I am a religious man. You may even say that I am superstitious. I believe that so long as you have not rid yourselves of this sin, have not begged forgiveness of the Antyajas, you will be visited with no end of misfortune. Know that the practice of untouchability is a sin. If you can, by your own voluntary effort; purge yourselves of the evils in you, you will have freedom for the asking.

I will cite another instance to show the flexibility of Hinduism. When I returned from South Africa, I had, accompanying me, a boy named Naidoo belonging to the Panchama community. Shri Natesan is a sincere worker in the cause of the Antyajas. Once I was to stay in his house when I was in Madras on my way to Ahmedabad. Many friends asked me if I knew what I was doing. Natesan's mother (they said) was so orthodox in her ideas that it would be death of the old lady to know that I was accompanied by an Antyajas boy. I told them that I would prefer to avoid Natesan's house rather than send away the boy elsewhere. Natesan, however, is a straightforward man. We went to his mother and told her the real fact. She said the boy was welcome. She had understood that a boy accompanying me could not lack cleanliness. I too had seen that he did not. We stayed in his house and drew our water from the very same well which the lady was using. What does this incident prove? That like Natesan, other caste Hindus can succeed, by the purity of their character and their straight forward-ness, in winning over their mothers and sisters. The point is that this problem can be solved only through the sincerity of caste Hindus and the *tapashcharya* of the Antyajas.

I pray to God to give wisdom and patience to the Antyajas so that they may not turn away from the path of *dharma*. On behalf of the Hindus, I pray to God that He may save Hindu society from this sin, from this Satanism.

Second Speech

It was hardly necessary to ask me to express my views on the subject of untouchability. I have declared times without number from various public platforms that it is the prayer of my heart that if I should fail to obtain *moksha* in this very birth I might be born a *Bhangi* in my next. I believe in *varnashrama* both according to birth and to *Karma*. But I do not regard *Bhangis* as in any sense a low order. On the contrary, I know many *Bhangis who* are worthy of reverence. On the other hand, there are Brahmins going about whom it would be very difficult to regard with any reverence. Holding these views, therefore, if there is a rebirth in store for me, I wish to be born a pariah in the midst of pariahs, because thereby I would be able to render more effective service to them and also be in a better position to plead with other communities on their behalf.

But just as I do not want the so-called touchables to despise the untouchables, so also I do not want the latter to entertain any feeling of hatred and ill will towards the former. I do not want them to wrest their right by violence as is done in the West. The trend of world opinion is against such violence. I can clearly see a time coming in the world when it will be impossible to secure rights by arbitrate of force, so I tell my untouchable brethren today as I tell the Government, that if they resort to force for the attainment of their purpose they shall certainly fail.

I want to uplift Hinduism. I regard the untouchables as an integral part of the Hindu community. I am pained when I see a single *Bhangi* driven out of the fold of Hinduism. But do not believe that all class distinctions can be obliterated. I believe in the doctrine of equality as taught by Lord Krishna in the 'Gita'. The 'Gita' teaches us that members of all the four castes should be treated on an equal basis. It does not prescribe the same *dharma* for the *Brahmin* as for the *Bhangi*. But it insists that the latter shall be entitled to the same measure of consideration and esteem as the former with all his superior learning. It is, therefore, our duty to see that the untouchables do not feel that they are despised or looked down upon. Let them not be offered leavings from our plates for their subsistence. How can I accord differential treatment to any person, be he *Brahmin* or *Bhangi*, who worships the same God, keeps his body and soul pure and clean? I for one would regard myself as having sinned if I gave, to an unclean, food from the leavings from the kitchen or failed to render him personal assistance when he was in need.

Let me make my position absolutely clear. While I do hold that the institution of untouchability as it stands today has no sanction in Hinduism, Hinduism does recognize "untouchability" in limited sense and under certain circumstances. For instance, every time that my mother handled unclean things she became untouchable by reason of his/her birth, and such untouchability as recognised by religion is by its very nature transitory, easily, removable and referable to the deed not the doer. Not only that. Just as we revere our mother for the sanitary service that she renders us when we are infants, and the greater her service the greater is our reverence for her, similar service they perform for society.

Now another point. I do not regard inter-dining and intermarriage as essential to the removal of untouchability. I believe in *Varnashrama dharma*. But I eat with *Bhangis*. I do not know whether I am a *sannyasi*, for I seriously doubt whether in this *Kaliyuga* it is at all possible for anyone to fulfill the conditions prescribed for a *sannyasi*. But I am moving deliberately in the direction of *sannyasa*. It is, therefore, not only necessary for me to observe these restrictions but their observance may be even harmful for me. As regards the question of intermarriage, it does not arise in case like mine. Sufficient for me to say that my scheme does not include intermarriage. Let me tell you that in my own clan all the members do not inter-dine. In certain cases among our *Vaishnava* families they do not use each other's utensils or even cook food on fire fetched from other's kitchens. You may call this practice superstitious, but I do not regard it as such. It certainly does no harm to Hinduism. In my Ashram, Dudhabhai, one of the untouchable inmates, dines with the rest without any distinction. But I do not recommend anybody outside the Ashram to follow this example. Again, you know the esteem in which I hold Malaviyaji. I would wash his feet. But he would not take food touched by me. Am I to resent it as a mark of contempt? Certainly not, because I know that no contempt is meant.

The religion to which I belong prescribes for our observance *maryada dharma*. The *rishis* of old carried on exhaustive researches through meditation, and as a result of the researches they discovered some great truths, such as have no parallel perhaps in any other religion. One of these was that they regarded certain kinds of foods as injurious for the spiritual well-being of man. So they interdicted their use. Now suppose someone had to travel abroad and live among strange people with different customs and standards as regard their diet. Knowing as they did how compelling some-times the force of social customs of the people among whom men lived was, they promulgated *maryada dharma* to help one in such emergencies. Though however, I believe in *maryada dharma*, I do not regard it as an essential part of Hinduism. I can even conceive a time when these restrictions might be abolished with impunity. But the reform contemplated in the untouchability movement does not obliterate the restriction as to inter-dining and intermarriage. I cannot recommend wholesale abolition of these restrictions to the public, even at the risk of being charged with hypocrisy and inconsistency. For instance, I let my son dine freely in Mussalman households because I believe he can take sufficient care as to what to take and what not to take. I myself have no scruples in taking my food in Mussalman households because I have my own strict rules about my diet. Let me tell you of an incident that happened at Aligarh. Swami Satyadev and I were Khwaja Sahib's guests. Swami Satyadev did not share my views. We argued about them. I told him that holding the views I did, it would be as wrong of me to refuse to partake of the food offered by a Mussalman as it would be on his part to transgress his maryada. So Swami Satyadev was provided with separate cooking arrangements. Similarly, when I was Bati Sahib's guest he provided us with a Brahmin cook with strict instructions to obtain all the rations for us fresh from the bazaar. When asked why he put himself to such inconvenience he explained that he did so become he wanted to avoid the slightest possibility of suspicion, on the part of the public that he entertained any secret designs of proselytization against me or my companions. That single incident raised Bari Sahib in my esteem. He sometimes commits mistakes, but he is as simple and innocent as a child. And although sometimes people complain of him to me bitterly my first impression of him still remains.

I have dwelt on this point at such great length, because I want to be absolutely plain with you (untouchables). I do not want to employ diplomacy in my dealings with you or for that matter with anyone. I do not want to keep you under any false illusion or win your support by holding out temptations. I want to remove untouchability because its removal is essential for *swaraj* and I want *Swaraj*. But I would not exploit you for gaining any political ends of mine. The issue with me is bigger even than *swaraj*. I am anxious to see an end put to untouchability because for me it is expiation and a penance. It is not the untouchables whose *shuddhi* I effect-the thing would be absurd- but my own and that of the Hindu religion. Hinduism has committed a great sin in giving sanction to this evil and I am anxious-if such a thing as vicarious penance is possible-to purify it of that sin by expiating for it in my own person. That being so, it follows that the only means open to me for my purpose are those of *ahimsa* and truth. I have adopted an untouchable child as my own. I confess I have not been able to convert my wife completely to my view. She cannot bring herself to love her as I do. But I cannot convert; my people have done you many wrong, I ask your forgiveness for it. Some members of the untouchable class said when I was at Poona that they would resort to force if the Hindus did not alter their attitude towards them. Can untouchability be removed by force? Can the amelioration of the untouchables come through these methods? The only way by which you and I can wean orthodox Hindus from their bigotry is by patient argument and correct conduct. So long as they are not converted, I can only ask you to put up with your lot with patience. I am willing to stand by you and share your sufferings with you. You must have the right of worship in any temple in which members of other castes are admitted. You must have admission to schools along with the children of other castes without any distinction. You must be eligible to the highest office in the land not excluding even that of the Viceroy's. That is my definition of the removal of untouchability.

But I can help you in this only by following the way indicated by my religion and not by following Western methods. For that way I cannot save Hinduism. Yours is a sacred cause. Can one serve a sacred cause by adopting Satan's methods? I pray you, therefore, to dismiss from your mind the idea of ameliorating your condition by brute force. The 'Gita' tell us that by sincerely meditating on the Lord in one's heart, one can attain *moksha* Meditation is waiting on God. If waiting on God brings the highest bliss of salvation, how much quicker must it bring removal of untouchability? Waiting on God means increasing purity. Let us by prayer purify ourselves and we shall not only remove untouchability but shall also hasten the advent of *Swaraj*.

CHAPTER-13

Cow-Protection

Cow-protection is an article of faith in Hinduism. Apart from its religious sanctity, it is an ennobling creed. But we, Hindus, have today little regard for the cow and her progeny. In no country in the world are cattle as ill-fed and ill-kept as in India. In beef-eating England it would be difficult to find cattle with bones sticking out of their flesh. Most of our *pinjrapoles* are ill-managed and ill-kept. Instead of being a real blessing to the animal world, they are perhaps simply receiving-depots for dying animals. We say nothing to the English in India for whose sake hundreds of cows are slaughtered daily. Our *rajas* do not hesitate to provide beef to their English guests. Our protection of the cow, therefore, extends to rescuing her from Mussulman hands. This reverse method of cow protection has led to endless feuds and bad blood between Hindus and Mussulmans. It has probably caused greater slaughter of cows than otherwise would have been the case if we had begun the propaganda in the right order. We should have commenced, as we ought now to commence, with ourselves and cover the land with useful propaganda leading to kindness in the treatment of cattle and scientific knowledge in the management of cattle farms, dairies and *pinjrapoles*. We should devote our attention to propaganda among Englishmen in the shape of inducing them voluntarily to abandon beef, or if they will not do so, at least be satisfied with imported beef. We should secure prohibition of export of cattle from India and we should adopt means of increasing and purifying our milk supply. I have not a shadow of doubt that if we proceed along these same lines, we would secure voluntary Mussulman support, and when we have ceased to compel them to stop killing cows on their festival days, we would find that they have no occasion for insisting on killing them. Any show of force on our part must lead to retaliation and exacerbation of feeling. We may not make Mussulmans or anybody respect our feelings religious or otherwise by force. We can really do so only by exciting their fellow-feeling.

Hence it is that I have declined, and I am sure quite wisely, to enter into any bargain on the khilafat question. I consider myself to be among the staunchest of Hindus. I am as eager to save the cow from the

Mussulman's knife as any Hindu. But on that very account I refuse to make my support of the Mussulman claim on the khilafat conditional upon his saving the cow. The Mussulman is my neighbour. He is in distress. His grievance is legitimate and it is my bounden duty to help him to secure redress by every legitimate means in my power, even to the extent of losing my life and property. That is the way I can win permanent friendship with Mussulmans. I refuse to suspect human nature. Its will is bound to, respond to any noble and friendly action. The nobility of the help will be rendered nugatory if it was rendered conditionally. That the result will be the saving of the cow is a certainty. But should it turn out to be otherwise, my view will not be affected in any manner whatsoever. The test of friendship is a spirit of love and sacrifice independent of expectation of any return.

But one observes a spirit of impatience on the part of the Hindus. In our eagerness to protect the cow we seek to legislate through municipalities and get the resolutions passed by Mussulman meetings. I would urge my Hindu countrymen to be patient. Our Mussulman countrymen are themselves doing most handsomely in the matter. I remind the readers of Maulana Abdul Bari's declaration that he could not take any preferred aid unless he, a devout Mussulman, could see his way clear to asking his followers to protect the cow. He has been as good as his word. He has been unremittingly attempting to create a favourable atmosphere for receiving the doctrine of cow protection on humanitarian and utilitarian grounds. Hakimjee Ajmalkhan as President of the Muslim League last year carried his resolution of abstention from cow-killing on festival days in the teeth of opposition members. The Ali Brothers have stopped beef-eating in their household. We must feel deeply grateful to those noble-hearted Mussulmans for their unsolicited response. We must let them solve the difficult problem in their own way. My advice to my Hindu brethren is, "simply help the Mussulmans in their sorrow in a generous and self-sacrificing spirit without counting the cost and you will automatically save the cow." Islam is a noble faith. Trust it and its followers. We must hold it a crime for any Hindu to talk to them about cow protection or any other help in our religious matters whilst the khilafat struggle is going on.

The cause of cow-protection is very dear to me. If someone were to ask me what the most important outward manifestation of Hinduism was, I would suggest that it was the idea of cow-protection. It has been clear to me for many years past that we have forsaken this duty. I have seen no country in the world where the progeny of the cow is as ill-fed and ill-cared for as in India. We do not find anywhere else such large numbers of cattle with bones sticking out of their flesh as we do in India. In England, the people actually eat beef, but I did not see in those country cattle which were ill-fed and ill-kept.

We are weak as our cattle are. It is not surprising to find three crores dying of hunger where the cattle are in similar plight.

Look at the condition of our *pinjrapoles*. I have respect for the kindness of the managers, but I have very little respect of their capacity for managing things. I do not believe that the *pinjrapoles* protect cows and their progeny. They should not be places where ill-fed and ill-kept cattle may be looked after and allowed to die peacefully. I would expect to see in them ideal cows and bulls. *Pinjrapoles* should be located, not in the heart of cities but in big fields and they should bring, instead of consuming, plenty of money.

How do the Hindus look after the cattle in the country? Are they not Hindus who goad them with sharpened nails on sticks, who put unbearable loads on them, keep them without enough fodder and make them work more than they can?

It is my firm conviction that the Hindus' first duty is to put their own house in order. I would, if I could and had necessary time at my disposal, engage the various cow-protection bodies in reforming the *pinjrapoles*, in imparting to the people scientific knowledge of cattle-breeding, in teaching cruel Hindus to have compassion for their cattle and in making available pure milk to the poorest child and to the sick. And I would first ask the Hindus to take charge of the gigantic task of organizing such bodies.

And then I would request the Englishmen to give up beef-eating. The princes forget, when entertaining English guests, the duty (of cow-protection) which is especially theirs and do not hesitate to order beef for them; I would request them to save themselves from this violation of their *dharma*, I would shame them into doing so.

Only after I have done this may I be entitled to ask my Muslim friends to stop cow-slaughter. Our duty, thus, is clear enough, but we have taken up the last thing first We seem to think that all we need to do by way of cow-protection is to save cows from the hands of Muslims, either with their goodwill or with force. As a result, the hostility between Hindus and Muslims has increased, a cause for discord has been created and the effort (to save cows in this manner) has led to their slaughter in increased numbers, for the thing became a point of honour with the Muslims. Our supreme duty is to lay down our lives for saving the cow.

Today, however, we have an invaluable opportunity and I have embraced it. Every Hindu can do the same thing and easily ensure the protection of cows. A great misfortune has befallen the Muslims, their religion has been slighted. At such a time, we should help them unconditionally, without asking for anything in return. It is our duty as neighbours to do this. The man who does his duty gets his reward, whether he hopes for it or not. By doing our duty to the Muslims, we challenge their nobility. Friendship which asks for a reward is no friendship, it is bargaining. If, at this juncture, we give up all thought of bargaining and help the Muslims, we shall ensure (cow) protection of their own freewill.

Some persons argue that in this matter Muslims cannot be trusted. I, for one, believe in human nature; I have faith in Islam. It is a divine law that nobility will be answered by nobility. It is only when our motives are mixed that we see contrary results. Even today, Muslims on their own have been doing much. Maulana Abdul Bari accepted my help only when he could find in his religion sanction for refraining from killing cows. Hakim Ajmal Khan is working hard for their protection. The Ali Brothers have banished beef from their homes altogether.

Let us not, by our suspicions or our impatience, endanger the change which is taking place.

I observe at some places a movement for legislation to ban cow-slaughter. Everywhere I hear people suggesting that we make conditions with Muslims. In both these, I see nothing but harm. Orthodox Hindus have only one thing to do at present and that is, to discharge, quietly, the duty, which is morally theirs, of helping Muslims. That is the way to ensure complete protection of the religion and honour of either.

The issue of cow-protection is intimately connected with the problem of Hindu-Muslim unity. But we will not consider it today from this point of view. There is much that I want to write about Hindu-Muslim unity and its bearing on the issue of cow-protection. But that can wait. Nor will we consider the question from the religious point of view. We shall discuss it exclusively from the economic standpoint.

I wish only to place before my readers some of my experiences during my stay here in the quiet of Juhu and the *old* ideas of mine that they revived. I have invited some persons who live with me or have been brought up by me or have been close to me, persons who have been ill for some time, to share with me the benefits of change of air. Their diet is mainly cow's milk. We found it rather difficult to obtain it here. There are in the vicinity three suburbs of Bombay, viz., Vile Parle, Andheri and Santa Cruz. Cow's milk was very difficult to obtain from any of these places. Buffalo's milk was plentiful. But even that could be had without adulteration only because of friends in the neighbourhood who are solicitous about my needs. Otherwise, pure milk of even buffaloes would be hard to come by. Ultimately, through God's grace and the kindness of friends, I could even get cow's milk. My friends tell me that they send me what they can spare, but I fear that I am, in fact, depriving them of what they need. Not everyone, however, may be as fortunate as I am. Though I persuade myself that I live like a beggar, there is no convenience that I do not enjoy. How far I deserve the unbounded love of my friends will only be known if some person, in his kindness, makes up an honest account after my death.

But this non-availability of cow's milk has again set me thinking. In India, a country in which live countless people whose religion enjoins love for all living creatures, where there are crores of zealous Hindus who venerate the cow as mother, how is it that it is only here in India that cows are in a wretched condition, that their milk is scarce, that such milk as is available is adulterated, and that milk of any sort is beyond the reach of the poor? For this, neither the Muslims nor British Rule can be blamed. If anyone is at fault, it is the Hindus, and even their indifference is not deliberate but the result of ignorance.

There are goshalas in every part of the country and they are all in a pitiable state. Here, too, the cause is simple inefficiency. Enormous amounts are spent on these *goshalas* or *pinjrapoles*. Some people say that this stream is also drying up. Be it so. I am convinced nonetheless that, if these institutions are established on a sound footing, devoted Hindus will pour money to help them. I am sure that the task is not impossible.

Pinjrapoles should be located on extensive grounds outside the city. They should house not only aged animals but milk cattle as well, so that pure milk needed by the city could be supplied from them. Many people who do not know me have often misrepresented me, and amused me too, by saying that I am against machines. I promise not to raise my *Mahatma's* voice against any machines that may be required for these milk centers. I will be, on the contrary, ready to lend them my humble support. If no Indian can be found to administer such a centre, I shall be entirely willing to have an Englishman appointed to that post. If in this way we can convert a *pinjrapole* into a milk centre, breed the best cattle and sell milk and butter at low prices, thousands of animals will be made happy and poor people and children will get pure ghee cheap. Eventually, every such *goshala* will become self-supporting or nearly so. If this experiment is tried in even one *goshala*, it will be possible to test the practicability of my scheme.

I hope that no one will raise the question: "But how does religion come into this? Is it not trade?" If there is any such skeptical reader, I would tell him that religion and affairs of practical life need not be mutually exclusive. When a certain practice is found to be contrary to religion, it should be abandoned. Religion, too, is truly tested only when it is followed in daily life. It demands more than ordinary efficiency, for without discrimination, thoughtfulness and other like qualities, religion cannot be followed in practice at all. At the present day, many rich people who are totally engrossed in the pursuit of wealth contribute, in their simple-mindedness, to all manner of funds without giving any thought; to the matter. Those in charge of the management of the institutions which become the victims of such contributions run them in an unimaginative way and we then proceed to give them our support. Thus, all the three parties deceive themselves and believe that they are doing good. The truth is that what is thus done in the name of *dharma* is often the very opposite of *dharma*. If these three parties use their discretion and understand *dharma* properly and follow it, or even if one party does so, every institution will breathe the true spirit of *dharma*.

Save the Cow

Professor Vaswani has unfurled the banner of the cow's freedom. The danger has come sooner than I had expected. I had hoped that it would come when India could regard it with equanimity. In my humble opinion, Professor Vaswani might have started the movement under better auspices. Any movement started by Hindus for protecting the cow, without whole-hearted Mussulman co-operation is doomed to failure.

The Hindus' participation in the Khilafat is the greatest and the best movement for cow-protection. I have therefore called *Khilafat* our *Kamadhuk*.

The Mussulmans are striving their utmost to respect Hindu susceptibilities in this matter of life and death to the Hindu. The Muslim League under Hakim Ajmal Khan's presidentship carried a cow-protection resolution at Amritsar two years ago. Maulana Abdul Bari has written upon it. The Ali Brothers, for the sake of their Hindu countrymen, have given up the use of beef in their house. Mian Chhotani saved hundreds of cows in Bombay alone during the last Bakr-i-Id. We could not accuse our Mussulman countrymen of apathy in the matter.

The surest way of defeating our object is to rush Mussulmans. I do not know that Mussulman honour has ever been found wanting. With them, as with everyone, prejudices die hard. We have got enlightened

Mussulman opinion with us. It must take time for it to react upon the Mussulman masses. The Hindus must, therefore, be patient.

There is nothing strange about all the Shikaspur Hindus having voted unanimously in favour of the prohibition of cow-slaughter. Is there a Hindu who will not vote for it? The use of that unanimous opinion for bearing down Mussulman opposition is the way to stiffen it The Hindu members must have known, must have ascertained, Mussulman feeling. And they should have refrained from going to a division, so long as the Mussulman opinion was against them.

Let us recognize that there is an interest actively working to keep us-Hindus and Mussulmans-divided, that very interest is quite capable of developing regard for Hindu susceptibilities in this respect. I should beware of it, and distrust it. I strongly advise the Shikarpur friends to wait for their Mussulman brethren.

Let them, by all means, abstain from all meat, so that their Mussulman brethren may have other meat cheaper than beef. Let them consider it a shame to have a single cow or her progeny in distress, or undergoing ill-treatment at the hands of Hindus themselves. Let them develop their *Goshala* so as to make it a model dairy farm as well as a home for aged and infirm cattle. Let them breed the finest cattle in their *Goshala*. They will do real service to *Gomata*. Let the Shikar-puris one and all become true non-cooperators, and hasten the redress of the Khilafat wrong. I promise they will save the cow when they have done their utmost to save the *Khilafat*.

It must be an article of faith for every Hindu that the cow can only be saved by Mussulman friendship. Let us recognize frankly that complete protection of the cow depends purely upon Mussulman goodwill. It is as impossible to bend the Mussulmans to our will as it would be for them to bend us to theirs. We are evolving the doctrine of equal and free partnership. We are fighting Dyerism-the doctrine of frightfulness.

Cow-protection is the dearest possession of the Hindu heart. It is the one concrete belief common to all Hindus. No one who does not believe in cow-protection can possibly be a Hindu. It is a noble belief. I endorse every word of what Professor Vaswani has said in praise of the cow. Cow-worship means to me worship of innocence. For me, the cow is the personification of innocence. Cow-protection means the protection of the weak and the helpless. As Professor Vaswani truly remarks, cow-protection means brotherhood between man and beast. It is a noble sentiment that must grow by patient toil and *tapasya*. It cannot be imposed upon anyone. To carry cow-protection at the point of a sword is a contradiction in terms. *Rishis* of old are said to have performed penance for the sake of the cow. Let us follow in the footsteps of the *rishis*, and ourselves do penance, so that we may be pure enough to protect the cow and all that the doctrine means and implies.

I hold the question of cow-protection to be not less momentous but in certain respects even of far greater moment than that of *swaraj*. I would even go so far as to say that just as so long as Hindu-Muslim unity is not effected, Hinduism not purged of the taint of untouchability and the wearing of hand-spun and hand-woven *khaddar* does not become universal, *swaraj* would be impossible of attainment: even so, the term "*swaraj*" would be devoid of all meaning so long as we have not found out a way of saving the cow, for that is the touchstone on which Hinduism must be tested and proved before there can be any real *swaraj* in India. I claim to be a *Sanatan* Hindu. People may laugh and say that to call myself a *sanatani* Hindu when I eat and drink from the hands of Mussalmans and Christians, keep an untouchable girl in my house as my daughter and do not even hesitate to quote the Bible, is nothing short of doing violence to language. But I would still adhere to my claim, for I have faith in me which tells me that a day would come-may be most probably after I am dead and no longer present in this world in the flesh to bear witness-when my critics would recognize their error and admit the just-ness of my claim. Pretty long while ago, I once wrote in *Young India* an article on Hinduism, which I consider to be one of my most thoughtful writings on the subject. The definition of Hinduism which I gave in it is probably the clearest that I have ever given. After defining a Hindu as one who believed in the Vedas and Upanishads, recited the *Gayatri* and subscribed to the doctrine of rebirth and transmigration, etc., I added that so far as the popular notion of Hinduism was concerned, its distinguishing feature was belief in cow-protection and reverence for the cow. I do not want to be told as to what Hindus ten thousand years ago did. I know there are scholars who tell us that cow-sacrifice is mentioned in the Vedas. I remember when I was a high school student we read a sentence in our Sanskrit text-book to the effect that the Brahmins of old used to eat beef. That exercised my mind greatly and I used to wonder and ask myself whether what was written could be after all true. But as I grew up the conviction slowly forced itself upon me that even if the text on which these statements were based was actually part of the Vedas, the interpretation put upon it could not be correct. I had conceived of another way out of the difficulty. This was purely for personal satisfaction. "If the *Vedic* text under reference was incapable of bearing any other interpretation than the literal," I said to myself, "the Brahmins who were alleged to be eating beef had the power to bring the slaughtered animals back to life again." But that is neither here nor there: The speculation does not concern the general mass of the Hindus. I do not claim to be a Vedic scholar. I have read Sanskrit scriptures largely in translation. A layman like myself, therefore, can hardly have any *locus standi* in a controversy like this. But I have confidence in myself. Therefore I do not hesitate to freely express to others my opinions based on my inner experience. It may be that we may not be all able to agree as to the exact meaning and significance of cow-protection. For Hinduism does not rest on the authority of one book or one prophet; nor does it possess a common creed-like the Kalma of Islam-acceptable to all. That renders a common definition of Hinduism a bit difficult, but therein lies strength also. For, it is this special feature that has given to Hinduism its inclusive and assimilative character and made its gradual, silent evolution possible. Go to any Hindu child and he would tell you that cow-protection is the supreme duty of every Hindu and that anyone who does not believe in it deserves the name of a Hindu.

But while I am a firm believer in the necessity and importance of cow-protection, I do not at all endorse the current methods adopted for that purpose. Some of the practices followed in the name of cow-protection cause me extreme anguish. My heart aches within me. Several years ago I wrote in *Hind Swaraj* that our cow-protection societies were in fact so many cow-killing societies. Since then and after my return to India in 1915, that conviction of mine has grown stronger and firmer everyday. Holding the views that I do, therefore, I have naturally felt a great hesitation in accepting the Presidentship of this Conference. Would it be proper for me to preside over this Conference under these circumstances? Would I at all succeed in convincing you of the soundness of my views—radically different as they are from the commonly accepted notions on this subject? These were the questions that I might preside over the Conference on my terms that Sjt. Chikodi was familiar with my views on the matter and was at one with me to a very large extent. So much by way of personal explanation.

Once, while in Champaran, I was asked to expound my views regarding cow-protection. I told my Champaran friends then that if anybody was really anxious to save the cow, he ought once for all to disabuse his mind of the notion that he had to make the Christians and Mussalmans to desist from cow-killing. Unfortunately today we seem to believe that the problem of cow-protection consists merely in preventing non-Hindus, especially Mussalmans, from beef-eating and cow-killing. That seems to me to be absurd. Let no one, however, conclude from this that I am indifferent when a non-Hindu kills a cow or that I can bear the practice of cow-killing. On the contrary, no one probably experiences a greater agony of the soul when a cow is killed. But what am I to do? Am I to fulfill my *dharma* myself or am I to get it fulfilled by proxy? Of what avail would be my preaching *brahmacharya* to others if I am at the same time steeped in vice myself? How can I ask Mussalmans to desist from eating beef when I eat it myself? But supposing even that I myself do not kill the cow, is it any part of my duty to make the Mussalman, against his will, to do likewise? Mussalmans claim that Islam permits them to kill the cow. To make a Mussalman, therefore, to abstain from cow-killing under compulsion would amount in my opinion to converting him to Hinduism by force. Even in India under *swaraj*, in my opinion, it would be for a Hindu majority unwise and improper to coerce by legislation a Mussalman minority into submission to statutory prohibition of cow-slaughter. When I pledge myself to save the cow, I do not mean merely the Indian cow, but the cow all the world over. My religion teaches me that I should by my personal conduct instil into the minds of those who might hold different views, the conviction that cow-killing is a sin and that therefore it ought to be abandoned. My ambition is no less than to see the principle of cow-protection established throughout the world. But that requires that I should set my own house thoroughly in order first.

Let alone other provinces. Would you believe me if I told you that the Hindus of Gujarat practise cow-killing? You will wonder but let me tell you that in Gujarat the bullocks employed for drawing carts are goaded with spiked rods till blood oozes from their bruised backs. You may say that this is not cow-killing but bullock-killing. But I see no difference between the two, the killing of the cow and killing her male progeny. Again you may say that this practice may be abominable and worthy of condemnation but it hardly amounts to killing. But here, again, I beg to differ. If the bullock in question had a tongue to speak and were asked which fate he preferred-instantaneous death under the butcher's knife or the long-drawn agony to which he is subjected, he would undoubtedly prefer the former. At Calcutta, a Sindhi gentleman used to meet me often. He used always to tell me stories about the cruelty that was practised by milkmen on cows in Calcutta. He asked me to see for myself the process of milking the cows as carried on in the dairies. The practice of blowing is loathsome. The people who do this are Hindus. Again, nowhere in the world is the condition of cattle so poor as in India. Nowhere in the world would you find such skeletons of cows and bullocks as you do in our cow-worshipping India. Nowhere are bullocks worked so beyond their capacity as here. I contend that so long as these things continue we have no right to ask anybody to stop cow-killing. In Bhagavata, in one place the illustrious author describes the various things which have been the cause of India's downfall: one of the causes mentioned is that we have given up cow-protection. Today I want to bring home to you if I can the close relation which exists between the present poverty stricken condition of India and our failure to protect the cow. We, who live in cities, probably can have no idea of the extent of the poverty of our poor folk. Millions upon millions cannot afford to have two full meals per day. Some live on rotten rice only. There are others for whom salt and chilies are the only table luxuries. Is it not a just nemesis for belying of our religion? Then in India we have the system of *pinjrapoles*. The way in which most of these are managed is far from satisfactory. And yet, I am sorry to observe that the people who are mostly responsible for them are Jains, who are out and out believers in *ahimsa*. Well organized, these *pinjrapoles* ought to be flourishing dairies supplying pure good milk at a cheap rate to the poor. I am told however, that even in a rich city like Ahmedabad there are cases of the wives of labourers feeding their babies on flour dissolved in water. There cannot be a sadder commentary on the way in which we protect the cow than that in a country which has such an extensive system of *pinjrapoles* the poor should experience a famine of pure, good milk. That I hope will serve to explain to you how our failure to protect the cow at one end of the chain results in our skin and bones traveling at the other.

If, therefore, I am asked how to save the cow, my first advice will be: "Dismiss from your minds the Mussalmans and Christian's altogether and mind your own duty first." I have been telling Maulana Shaukat Ali all along that I was helping him to save his cow, i.e., the Khilafat, because I hoped to save my cow thereby. I am prepared to place my like in the hands of the Mussalmans, to live merely on their sufferance. Why? Simply that I might be able to protect the cow. I hope to achieve the end not by entering into a bargain with the Mussalmans but by bringing about a change of heart in them. So long as this is not done I hold my soul in patience. For I have not a shadow of doubt in my mind that such a change of heart can be brought about only by our own correct conduct towards them and by our personal example.

Cow-slaughter and man-slaughter are in my opinion the two sides of the same coin. And the remedy for both is identical, i.e., that we develop the *ahimsa* principle and endeavour to win over our opponents by love. The test of love is *tapasya* and *tapasya* means suffering. I offered to share with the Mussalmans their suffering to the best of my capacity not merely because I wanted their co-operation for winning *swaraj* but also because I had in mind the object of saving the cow. The Koran, so far as I have been able to understand it, declares it to be a sin to take the life of any living being without cause. I want to develop the capacity to convince the Mussalmans that to kill the cow is practically to kill their fellow-countrymen and friends-the Hindus. The Koran says that there can be no heaven for one who sheds the blood of an innocent neighbour. Therefore I am anxious to establish the best neighbourly relations with the Mussalmans. I scrupulously avoid doing anything that might hurt their feelings. I even try to respect their prejudices. I do this not in a spirit of bargain, I ask them for no reward. For that I look to God only. My 'Gita' tells that evil can never result from a good action. Therefore I must help the Mussalmans from a pure sense of duty without making any terms with them. For more cows are killed today for the sake of Englishmen in India than for the Mussalmans. I want to convert the former also. I would like to convince them that whilst they are in our midst their duty lies in getting rid of their Western culture to the extent that it comes in conflict with ours. You will thus see that even our self- interest requires us to observe *ahimsa*. By *ahimsa* we will be able to save the cow and also to win the friendship of the English. I want to purchase the friendship of all by sacrifice. But if I do not approach the English on bent knees, as I do the Mussalmans that is because the former are intoxicated with power. The Mussalman is a fellow sufferer in slavery. We can therefore speak to him as a friend and a comrade. The Englishman, on the contrary, is unable to appreciate our friendly advances. He would spurn them. He does not care for our friendship, he wants to patronize us. We want neither his insults nor his patronage. We therefore let him alone. Our *Shastras* have laid down that charity should be given only to a deserving person, that knowledge should be imparted only to one who is desirous of having it. So we content ourselves with non-cooperating with our rulers-not out of hatred but in a spirit of love. It was because love was the motive force behind non-cooperation that I advised suspension of civil disobedience when violence broke out in Bombay and Chauri Chaura. I wanted to make it clear to Englishmen that I wanted to win *swaraj* not by shedding their blood but by making them feel absolutely at ease as regards the safety of their persons. What profit would it be if I succeed in saving a few cows from death by using force against persons who do not regard cow-killing as sinful? Cow-protection then can only be secured by cultivating universal friendliness, i.e., *ahimsa*. Now you will understand why I regard the question of cow- protection as greater even than that of *swaraj*. The fact is that the capacity to achieve the former will suffice for the latter purpose as well.

So far I have confined myself to the grosser or material aspect of cow-protection, i.e, the aspect that refers to the animal cow only. In its finer or spiritual sense the term cow-protection means the protection of every living creature. Today the world does not fully realize the force and possibilities that He hidden in *ahimsa*. The scriptures of Christians Mussalmans and Hindus are all replete with the teaching of *ahimsa*. But we do not know its full import. The *rishis* of old performed terrible penances and austerities to discover the right meaning of sacred texts. Today we have at least two interpretations of the *Gayatri*. Which one of them is correct, that of the *sanatanis* or that of the Arya Samajists? Who can say? But our *rishis* made the startling discovery (and every day I feel more and more convinced of its truth) that sacred texts and inspired writings yield their truth only in proportion as one has advanced in the practice of *ahimsa* and truth. The greater the realization of truth and *ahimsa* the greater the illumination. These same *rishis* declared that cow- protection was the supreme duty of a Hindu and that its performance brought one *moksha*, i.e., salvation. Now I am not ready to believe that by forcibly protecting the animal cow, one can attain *moksha* For *moksha* one must completely get rid of one's lower feelings like attachment hatred, anger, jealousy, etc. It follows, therefore, that the meaning of cow-protection in terms of *moksha* must be much wider and far more comprehensive than is commonly supposed. The cow-protection which can bring one *moksha must*, from its very nature, include the protection of everything that feels. Therefore, in my opinion, every little breach of the *ahimsa* principle, like causing hurt by harsh speech to anyone, man woman or child, to cause pain to the weakest and the most insignificant creature on earth would be a breach of the principle of cow protection would be tantamount to the sin of beef-eating, differing from it in degree, if at all, rather than in kind. That being so, I hold that with all our passions let loose we cannot today claim to be following the principle of cow-protection.

At Lahore, I met Lala Dhanpatrai, somewhat of a crank like myself. He told me that if I wanted to save the cow I should wean the Hindus from their false notions. He said it was Hindus who sold cows to the Mussalman butcher and but for them, the latter would have no cows to kill. The reason for this practice he told me was economical. The village commons that served as grazing grounds for the cattle had been enclosed by the Government and so people could not afford to keep cows. He suggested a way out of the difficulty. It was no longer necessary, he told me, to sell cows that had ceased to give milk. He then put them to the plough. After some time, if proper care was taken they put on flesh and became fit to bear again. I cannot vouch for the truth of this statement.

But I see no reason why this practice should not be generally adopted if the facts are as stated by Lala Dhanpatrai. Our Shastras certainly have nowhere said that under no circumstances should the cow not be used for draught purposes. If we feed the cow properly, tend it carefully and then use her for drawing carts or working the plough, always taking care not to tax her beyond her capacity, there can be nothing wrong in it. I therefore commend the suggestion for consideration and adoption if it is found to be workable. We may not look down upon a person if he tries to protect the cow in this manner.

CHAPTER-14

Power of Ramanama

A correspondent asks the following question:

I do not know the writer. The fact that he had the letter delivered to me through his brother when I was leaving Bombay shows the strength of his curiosity in this matter. Ordinarily, such questions should not be discussed in public. It is evident that, if it became the general practice with the public to probe into the private life of an individual, most unpleasant results would follow. But I cannot escape being the object of such curiosity, whether it is worthy or unworthy. I have no right to try to escape. Neither do I wish to do so. My private life has become public life. For my part there is not a single thing in the world which I would conceal from others. My experiments are spiritual. Some of them are novel. They depend very much on self-examination on my part. I have carried them out, following the maxim: "As in one's body, so in the universe". The underlying assumption is that what is possible to me must be so to all others. Hence I have to answer some questions about private matters too.

Moreover, I cannot resist the opportunity I have got, in answering this question, of explaining the power of *Ramanama*.

I should, however, like to request this correspondent and others who may put questions to me in future that, if they base their questions on newspaper reports, they should send me copies of the papers in question. I have often stated that I do not read newspapers for the simple reason that I am not able to do so. I do not know what Saurashtra has written. It is difficult to take notes of my speeches. Mahadevbhai does so, but I do not always, approve the notes he takes. The reason is that when subtle or new ideas are being expressed, an error in reporting even one word may misrepresent the speaker's meaning. Hence, when reporters who are not familiar with my ideas take notes of my speeches, they can never be relied upon, and I have often asked readers not to depend on such reports. When they have a doubt about anything, they may ask me and, while doing so, they should also send me a copy of the newspaper in which they have read reports of my speeches.

With these prefatory remarks, even though I do not know what Saurashtra has said on the matter, I shall describe how I was saved on those three occasions by the grace of God. All the three occasions concern public women. I was taken to two of them by friends on different occasions.

On the first occasion, I went to the place out of false regard for the friend and, if God had not saved me, I would certainly have fallen. This time the woman whose house I had entered herself threw me out with contempt. I simply did not know what to say or how to behave in such a situation. Prior to this incident I always regarded it as shameful even to sit near a public woman, so that I was trembling even when entering that house. After going in, I could not even look at her face and I do not know what her face was like. What could that smart woman do to such a fool but turn him out? She said a few angry words to me and asked me to go away. At that time, of course, I did not realize that God hid saved me. I left feeling miserable. I felt crest-fallen and even unhappy about my stupidity! I felt that I lacked manliness. It was later I realized that I had been shielded by my stupidity. God had saved me by making me behave like a fool. Else how could I, who had entered a house of ill-fame with evil intention, have been saved?

The second occasion was more dreadful than the first one. I was not so innocent then as I was at the time of the first incident, though I was, of course, more vigilant. Moreover, I had the protection of a vow administered to me by my revered mother. But this time the place was in England. I was in the very flush of youth. Two of us friends were lodged in one house. We had gone there only for a few days. The landlady was as good as a prostitute. Two or three of us sat down to play cards with her. In those days I used to play cards on occasion. In England a mother and a son can, and do, play cards for innocent amusement. On this occasion too, we sat down to play following the usual custom. The beginning was completely innocent. I, of course, did not know that the landlady lived on her body. But as the play warmed up, the atmosphere changed. The woman started making gestures. I was observing my friend. He had abandoned all restraints. I felt tempted. I was flushed in the face, for lust had entered me and I had become impatient.

But who can harm him whom Rama protects? To be sure, His name was not on my lips at that hour, but He ruled my heart. On my lips was the language of lust. My good friend noticed my behaviour. We knew each other very well. He had seen me in difficult situations in which I had, with an effort of will, kept my purity. But he saw that on this occasion evil had entered my mind and that, if the night progressed while I was in that mood, I too would fall like him.

It was this friend who first made me realize that even immoral men have good instincts. He felt unhappy to see me in that plight. I was younger than he. Rama came to my help through his person. He aimed arrows of love at me: "Moniya!" (This is an affectionate form of "Mohandas". I remember that I used to be called by that name by my mother, my father and the eldest cousin in our family. The fourth person to call me so was this friend who, through his goodness, proved a brother to me.) "Moniya, be careful. You know that I have fallen. But I shall not let you fall. Recall the promise you have made to your mother. This thing is not for you. Be off from here. Go to bed. Are you gone? Throw off the cards."

I do not remember whether I replied to him. I put down the cards. For a moment I felt unhappy I felt ashamed and my heart began to beat fast. I get up and went to bed.

I woke up. I started repeating the name of Rama. "How miraculously I have been saved, how He has saved me! All honour to my promise! All glory to my mother! All glory to my friend! All glory to Rama!" I kept saying to myself. For me, this was indeed a miracle. If my friend had not shot at me the invincible arrows of Rama, where would I have been today'!

He on whom Rama's arrows have lighted—
he knows what they are.
He on whom love's arrows have lighted—
he knows what they are.

For me, this was an occasion when I first became aware of the existence of God.

If today the whole of the world told me that there is no God, no Rama, I would say it lied. If I had fallen on that terrible night, I would not today be waging battles of *satyagraha*, would not be washing away the filth of untouchability, would not be repeating the holy name of the spinning-wheel, would not regard myself fit to be blessed by the *darshan* of millions of women, and would not be surrounded by hundreds of thousands of them who sit near me without fear as they sit around a child. I would always be running away from them, and they would have quite justifiably kept themselves at a distance from me. I look upon this occasion as the most perilous in my life. Seeking pleasure I learnt self- restraint. On the path to forsake Rama's name, I had his *darshan* A miracle indeed.

Oh scion of Raghu's race, protect my honour,
J am a fallen man, old in my evil ways;
Take my boat safely to the other shore.

The third incident is amusing. During one of my journeys, I came into fairly close contact with the ship's captain, as also with an English passenger. In every port where the ship weighed anchor, the captain and some passengers would go and search for brothels. The captain once invited me to go with him and see the port. I did not know what that meant. We went and stood before a prostitute's house. Then I knew what was meant by going to see a port. Three women were produced before us. I was completely taken aback, but felt too embarrassed to say anything: Nor could I run away. I had, of course, no wish to indulge in this immoral pleasure. Those two went into the rooms. The third woman led me into her own room. While I was still thinking what I should do, the other two came out of the rooms. I do not know what that woman must have thought about me. She stood smiling before me, but that did not have the slightest effect on me. Since we spoke different languages, there was no question of my talking to her. Those friends shouted for me and so I went out. I certainly felt a little humiliated. They had seen that I was a fool in these matters. They even joked between themselves on this point. They pitied me, of course. From that day, I was enrolled among the fools of the world, as far as the captain was concerned. He never invited me again to see a port. If I had remained in the room longer or if I had known that woman's language, I do not know what would have been my plight. But I certainly realized that day, too, I was not saved by my own power, but that it was God who had protected me by having made me stupid in such matters.

I remembered only these three incidents at the time of the speech in question. The reader should not think that I have not been through more of similar experiences. But I certainly wish to state that every time I escaped, thanks to *Ramanama* God gives the strength only to weak that approach Him in utter helplessness.

So long as the elephant trusted to his own strength,
So long his efforts availed him not.
Let the weak appeal to Rama's strength,
He will come to help
Before the name is uttered in full.

What, then, does this *Ramanama* mean? Is it something to be repeated parrot-like? Certainly not. If that were so, all of us would win deliverance by repeating it mechanically. *Ramanama* ought to be repeated from the depth of one's heart; it would not then matter if the words are not pronounced correctly. The broken words which proceed from the heart are acceptable in God's court. Even though the heart cries out "Mara, mara", this appeal of the heart will, be recorded in one's credit column.

On the contrary, though the tongue may pronounce the name of Rama correctly, if the lord of that heart is Ravana, the correct repetition of Rama's name will be recorded in one's debit column.

Tulsidas did not sing the glory of *Ramanama* for the benefit of the hypocrite who "has Rama's name on his lips and a knife under his arm." His wise calculations will go wrong, while the seeming errors of the man who has installed Rama in his heart will succeed. Rama alone can repair one's fortunes and so the poet Surdas, lover of God, sings:

Who will repair my fortunes?
O who else but Rama?
Everyone is a friend of his
On whom good fortune smiles,
None of his whom fortune has forsaken.

The reader, therefore, should understand clearly that *Ramanama* is a matter of the heart. Where speech and the mind are not in harmony with each other, mere speech is falsehood, no more than pretence or play words. Such chanting may well deceive the world, but can Rama who dwells in man's heart be deceived? Hanuman broke open the beads in the necklace which Sita gave him as a gift, wanting to see whether they were inscribed with Rama's name. Some courtiers who thought themselves wise asked him why he showed disrespect to Sita's necklace. Hanuman's reply was that, if the beads were not inscribed with Rama's name inside, then every necklace given to him by Sita was a burden to him. The wise courtiers thereupon smilingly asked him if Rama's name was inscribed in his heart. Hanuman drew out his knife and, cutting open his chest said: "Now look inside. Tell me if you see anything else there except Rama's name." The courtiers felt ashamed. Flowers rained on Hanuman from the sky, and from that day Hanuman's name is always invoked when Rama's story is recited.

This may be only a legend or a dramatist's invention. Its moral is valid for all time: only that which is in one's heart is true.

❍

CHAPTER-15

Ramanama and Khadi

"Juna Jogi" writes as follows:

This letter has been lying with me for two months. I had hoped, when I had leisure, to place it before the readers of *Navajivan*. I have found that leisure today or, rather, I have contrived to find it. The writer has advised me not to go fault finding. And let it not be said that I am finding fault with his letter if I happen to criticize it, for the motive behind my criticism is somehow to fit it into these pages so as to expound the glory of God. Let the writer and others know that I am adopting whatever in it is worth adopting. I feel I have nothing new to learn about the glory of *Ramanama* as I have realized it through experience. And hold that it cannot be propagated in the same manner as *khadi* or *swaraj*. In these very difficult times, even the utterance of the Name is done in a wrong way. In other words, I have heard it repeated often for mere show, sometimes for selfish ends and sometimes even in order to feed licentious conduct. There would be nothing to object to if one uttered "Mara" reversing the order of syllables, while chanting the Name. We read of the pure in heart having attained *mukti* even by chanting it in an erroneous manner and we can believe this too to be true. However, what are we to say of sinners who, although their pronunciation is perfect, chant the *mantra* of *Ramanama* in order to nourish their sins? That is why I am afraid of any propaganda for *Ramanama*. Those persons who believe that by sitting together in company and loudly repeating the Name they can wash away all their past, present and future sins and that nothing besides this shouting is expected of them, deserve to be bowed to from a distance. No one should imitate them. I, for my part, regard those who support and spread *khadi* etc., as being worthy of repeating *Ramanama* But repeating the Name, I find, has nowhere brought about an atmosphere congenial for the spread of *khadi*. How can a servant of Rama put it down in writing saying that no one in this world has been able to convert learned men? It does not seem to me that I am under any delusion. Learned persons too belong to the world of Rama and many of them have *attained* moksha by repeating His Name. The truth of the matter is that no one but a devotee can convert learned persons. And I who hope to become a devotee am ever trying to make these persons understand. And as I have no delusion, I am not angry with those who do not understand but rather with myself because my devotion is imperfect. Hence in order that Rama may forever dwell in my heart I welcome the advice that I should further purify my heart, and I constantly give myself such advice. It is the devotee who is to blame, not the listener, if he cannot make his devotion interesting. If the devotion has many attractive qualities, these will certainly be seized upon by the listener; however, is the listener to blame if he had found nothing interesting in it? If Krishna's flute had been a broken one and if the gopis had shrunk from the hush tunes coming out of it, Krishna would have been disgraced and no one would blame the gopis. Poor Arjuna was hardly aware of the fact that he was a mere hook-worm, or that he was making a false claim to learning. However, Krishna's clarity of vision enabled him to purify Arjuna's vision and cure him of his delusion. Hence, one who wishes to propagate Hamartoma should do so after convincing himself, purifying himself and, establishing Rama's kingdom in his own heart. To this, the world will respond and it will begin chanting His Name. However, to have it chanted anywhere and in any manner one likes is to bring disgrace to *Ramanama* by adding to the hypocrisy which is already there and accelerating the torrential current of atheism.

It is hardly possible for one today to stay in peace in one place. How can even Rama have any effect on one whose body is chained but whose mind constantly traverses across millions of miles? However, what can be said of the person who, like Damayanti searching for Nala, wanders from one forest to another, questions even the trees and animals of the whereabouts of Rama-should it be said of him that he is a wanderer or, should it be said that he stays in peace in one place? Can we not say rather that the real seer is he alone who has seen the seated one wandering around and the wanderer staying in one place? How can the duty that one has to perform be determined? Is it not determined simply by doing it? And, if this is true, I have conquered the world as I never ask anyone to do what I do not do myself. I have no alternative before me but to tell the reader of the delusion of this "Juna Jogi". Others may not know this, but the gentleman in question certainly knows that I have no such attendants who would hold back from me any letter, such as this one, which has been written in a friendly spirit. I received this letter promptly. Who is, however, to blame for my inability to reply to it for two months-those poor attendants, myself, fate, or the writer himself? Let us conclude that the writer himself is to blame. A person, who writes to me a letter which puts me into an extremely difficult dilemma, should certainly have the patience to wait for a reply. The problem that he has posed is not so simple that I could solve it instantly as I could point out that cloth made of mill spun yarn is not *khadi*. I was certainly afraid that, by replying to such a letter, I might impair the glory of *Ramanama*. Hence, I still feel that there was nothing wrong in not replying to it, and perhaps there is some delusion in this reply. However, even if there is, I place this reply at the feet of Rama in the same way as I would do some meritorious deed.

CHAPTER-16

The Hindu Widow

God created nothing finer than the Hindu widow. Whenever I hear men recounting their misfortunes, the picture of the widow comes vividly before my eyes and I laugh at the man who bewails his misfortunes.

Self-control has been carried by Hinduism to the greatest height and, in a widow's life, it reaches perfection. Man can find a remedy for his misfortunes, which are usually the consequence' of his own folly. Much of his misery is due merely to greed. But what of the widow? She, poor woman, is in no way responsible for her misfortune. Nor is the remedy for it open to her, for custom has barred that door. A great many widows do not even look on their suffering as suffering. Renunciation has become second nature to them, and to renounce it would be painful to them. They find happiness in their self-denial.

This is not an undesirable state On the contrary, it is good It is Hinduism at its best. I regard the widow's life as an ornament to Hinduism. When I see a widow, I instinctively bow my head in reverence. I never regard the sight of a widow as an ill omen. I feel blessed if I see the face of one in the morning. A widow's blessing is to me a gift which I prize. Seeing her, I forget all my sorrows. Man is but a clod before her. A widow's patient suffering is impossible to rival. Compared to her inheritance of ages, of what worth is a man's self-acquired wealth of brief renunciation?

If a widow suffers, before whom can she pour out her grief? If there is anyone in this world before whom she can do so, it is her mother. But what is the use? What help can the mother give? All she can do is to ask her to be patient and go and attend to her work. For a widow, her mother's house is no longer her home. She must live with her father-in-law's family. Only a daughter-in-law knows what it is to be harassed by a mother-in-law. A widow's duty is to serve others. The brother-in-law, the mother-in-law, the father-in-law and every chance visitor-she must serve them all. She is never weary. She only prays for strength to enable her to serve better.

If this holy life lived by widows becomes a thing of the past, if this living image of service is destroyed through ignorance or pride, incalculable harm will be done to Hinduism.

How can this way of life for widows be kept alive? What share of the virtues of following it can be claimed by parents who marry off a daughter only ten years old? Can the girl who becomes a widow on the very day she is married be regarded as a widow? Are we not committing an unforgivable sin by regarding as *dharma* the extreme length to which the rules about a widow's life are carried? If this way of life is to be kept alive, is it not essential that the men give thought to their own duty? Can a woman, who is innocent of what widowhood means, possess a body that can follow the widow's life? Who can imagine how a girl married today feels? What is her father's duty towards her? Or, was it over when he put a knife to her throat?

It is my humble opinion that the following rules are necessary for preserving the sanctity of the widow's life, for preserving Hinduism and for order in Hindu society.

1. No father should get a daughter under the age of 15 married.
2. If a girl below this age has already been married and has become a widow, it is the father's duty to get her married again.
3. If a fifteen-year-old girl becomes a widow within a year of her marriage, her parents should encourage her to marry again.
4. Every member of the family should look upon the widow with the utmost respect. Parents or parents-in-law must provide her with the means of improving her knowledge.

I have not suggested these rules to be generally followed. They are to serve only as a guide. I am convinced that our duty towards widows is along the lines indicated in them.

Who should ensure that these rules are followed? In Hindu society, castes are the natural agencies for this purpose. But till such time as they are reformed, what should those parents do who are ready to follow these rules? They should make efforts to persuade their community to introduce reforms and, if they do not succeed, free themselves from the shackles of the caste and search for a suitable bridegroom for the widow. Both the parties should be ready to live outside the caste and appeal to its members from outside. They should do nothing which would shock the leaders, nor should they think of resorting to *satyagraha*; if at all they want to offer *satyagraha*, they should understand that staying humbly outside the caste is in itself *satyagraha*. If the marriage had been thought of as the only possible course in the circumstances, if the motive behind it was to live a life of self-control and if the ostracized family's life is blameless in every way, then the elders will not only take them back into the caste, but will also accept this reform and other poor widows will be spared the torture which would have been theirs otherwise.

Such reforms cannot be brought about immediately, but 'it is enough if their seeds are sown. In time, the seeds will surely grow into trees.

I have suggested only a minor reform. I have done this because a really big reform may seem impossible. This reform would be that, man too, like woman, should not remarry after the death of his partner. If we understand the true meaning of Hinduism, we would not reduce the rigour of a restraint which is difficult to practice, but would, on the contrary, introduce in our lives other similar restraints and thus practice the former more rigidly. If widowers do not marry again, widows would not feel life to be a burden, and marriages of ill-matched pairs and of children, which are so common today would stop.

There is in all this one danger which we should guard against. I have heard the following argument: "The widow's customary life is a great ideal in every way. Why, then, bother to.get a few child widows remarried? We want even widowers to refrain from marrying again. Besides, we want the custom of child-marriage also to end. It is not necessary, therefore, to encourage widows to remarry under any circumstances." This is a dangerous argument, for it is mere sophistry. It resembles an argument put forward by some British friends: "You believe in nonviolence and want us also to practice non-violence. Hence, no matter what force we use, you ought not to ask your people to resist us with force." This is what some of them tell me. The fallacy in this reasoning is plain enough. All of us commit similar fallacies knowingly or unknowingly. The British friends who argue in this way forget that I wish to teach non-violence to both parties. But how can I advocate nonviolence to those who are incapable of understanding it, who are, in other words, cowardly? I could not convince my son of the duty of remaining non-violent. Nor could I get it accepted by the poor and harassed villagers of Bettiah. I had to tell them: "If your choice lies between running away and leaving a woman to her fate or defending her by force against a miscreant, if you cannot, resolutely, remain where you are and, looking upon him as your brother and using no force against him, oppose him with *satyagraha* unto death, then by all means attack him with force and defend the woman." The path of *satyagraha* is not for cowards. It is only when a person has shed his cowardice and become a man that he is fit for the method of non-violence.

If we now examine the sophistic argument in regard to widows, we shall see that only widowers who are ready to remain unmarried have a right to advance it. Others who do not appreciate the idea of a widower remaining unmarried or who, though they appreciate the idea itself, are not ready to act upon it, have no right to use that as an argument for defending the custom of compelling widows to remain unmarried Imagine a sixty-year-old man, who had remarried, cheerfully contemplating the possibility of his nine-year-old wife, so-called, becoming a widow, writing admiringly in his will about her state, saluting his poor child-wife doomed to be a widow and saying: "If, through misfortune, I die before my most virtuous wife, my partner in *dharma*, I know that she will remain a widow and shed glory on me, on my and her parents' families and on the Hindu way of life. Having married this girl, I have realized that a widower should remain unmarried. I would have done better if I had done so. I admit my weakness. But a man's weakness adds to the lustre of a widow's life. Concerning my child-wife, therefore, I desire that, after my death, she should remain a widow and illustrate the glory of self-control." What effect will this argument have on that child widow or on those who read the will?

It was necessary to examine this argument, since, under cover or in the name of loyalty to a noble ideal, many unholy practices which have the appearance of being holy are defended. The definition of a widow can have no reference to child marriages. A widow means a woman who, at the proper age, married a person of her choice or was married to him with her consent, who has had relations with her husband, and who has then lost her husband. A wife who has not known consummation of marriage or a girl of tender age sacrificed by her parents cannot and must not be included in this definition. It is, therefore, perversity to defend the custom forcing girls to submit to their so-called widowhood. But, when men advocate enforced widowhood for girls by admitting the necessity of widowers, too, remaining unmarried they add either impudence or profound ignorance to their perversity.

CHAPTER-17

How To Celebrate Diwali?

It would be no exaggeration to say that in this Kaliyuga we have no right to celebrate Diwali with so much jubilation. Our celebrating Diwali implies that we feel we are living in Ramarajya. Do we have Ramarajya in India today?

A king who is not prepared to listen to his subjects, under whose rule the subjects get no milk to drink, no food to eat and no cloth to wear, a king who massacres his innocent subjects, who trades in wine, hemp and opium, who, by eating pork, hurts the feelings of Muslims and by eating beef the feelings of Hindu, who threatens the very existence of Islam and gambles at horse racing-how can the subjects of such a king celebrate Diwali?

Let no one labour under the delusion that this is an exaggerated picture; if there is anyone who has such fear, I shall be only too happy to be able to explain the thing to him in all humility. If I am being in the least unfair to the British, I am ready to be convinced of my mistake and, on being convinced, I shall consider it my religious duty to apologize to them.

I would apply to any Indian Prince the standard I apply to the British Government. Actually, I apply a much stricter standard to Indian Princes. Judging it even by the lightest standard, I find British rule repugnant to me. All my admiration for this rule has vanished.

I have the utmost respect for the courage of the British. Their team spirit and organizing power are wonderful. Their literature has much that is admirable. Reading their Bible, I feel myself in bliss. However, their selfishness overshadows their fine qualities. Their activities have done nothing but harm to India. These policies have ruined and emasculated the country. I am convinced that never under Moghul rule, or at any other time, were the people so thoroughly emasculated as they are today. This is no accidental result but has been deliberately brought about, and so I look upon this rule as Ravanarajya. The government we dream of, I describe as Ramarajya. *Swaraj* alone can be such Ramarajya.

How may we establish it?

In former times, the subjects did *tapascharya* when they were oppressed. They believed that it was because of their sins that they got a wicked king and so they tried to purify themselves. The first step in this was to recognize a monster as such and avoid him, to non-cooperate with him. Even non-cooperation requires courage. To cultivate it, one needs to give up comforts and pleasures. To receive education provided by wicked Government, to accept honours at its hands, to seek settlement of one's disputes through its agency, to help it in framing laws, to provide it with policemen, to wear cloth produced by it, to do this while desiring that it should perish is like trying to cut off the branch on which one is sitting. This is nothing but sin. Nor, in this way, shall we succeed in destroying the Government. How, then, should we celebrate Diwali?

- If our children are attending Government schools, we should withdraw them from such schools.
- We should start other schools in their place.
- We should settle our disputes privately through *panchas*.
- If we are lawyers, we should give up practice.
- We should resolve, if we are voters, and persuade others, not to vote for any candidate. If anyone from our own locality stands as a candidate, we should send him a "card" requesting him to withdraw his candidature.
- We should introduce the sacred spinning-wheel in our homes.
- We should get hand-spun yarn woven into cloth and wear such cloth, bearing the additional burden for the sake of the country.

All these things need money, of course. We should, therefore, donate what we can and collect contributions from others. If the people listen to me, I would advise them to do nothing during the Diwali but engage themselves in work for *swaraj*.

This, at any rate, we should not do during Diwali:

Treat ourselves to pleasures,
Gamble,
Prepare all manner of sweet dishes, and
Enjoy ourselves with fire-works.

The money saved by renouncing these things, we should donate for *swaraj* work.

This is the duty dictated by these difficult times. When we have the

Government, of our dream, we may enjoy some innocent pleasures. At present, however, the people are in mourning, they are widowed. At such a time, they can have no celebrations.

CHAPTER-18

Who is a True Vaishnava?

A true *Vaishnava* is he-
Who is moved by others' sufferings;
Who helps people in distress?
And feels no pride for having done so.
Respectful to everyone in the world,
He speaks ill of none;
Is self-controlled in action, speech and thought—
Twice-blessed the mother who bore such a one.
He has an equal-seeing eye, and is free from all craving.
Another's wife is to him a mother;
His tongue utters no untruth,
And never his hand touches another's wealth
Moha and *maya* have no power over him,
In his mind reigns abiding detachment;
He dances with rapture to Rama's name-
No centre of pilgrimage but is present in his person-
A man he is without greed and cunning,
And purged of anger and desire;
Offering reverence to such a one, says Narasainyo,
Will bring release to seventy-one generations of
one's forbears.

From the marks of a *Vaishnava* described by Narasinh Mehta we see that he is a man who

- ⇨ is ever active in bringing relief to the distressed,
- ⇨ takes no pride in doing so,
- ⇨ is respectful to all,
- ⇨ speaks ill of none,

- ➪ is self-controlled in speech,
- ➪ in action and
- ➪ in thought,
- ➪ holds all in equal regard,
- ➪ has renounced desires.
- ➪ is loyal to one woman, his wife,
- ➪ is ever truthful,
- ➪ keeps the rule of non-stealing,
- ➪ is beyond the reach of maya
- ➪ is, in consequence, free from all desire,
- ➪ is ever absorbed in repeating Rama's name,
- ➪ and, as a result, has been sanctified,
- ➪ covets nothing,
- ➪ is free from guile,
- ➪ from the urge of desire, and
- ➪ from anger.

Here Narasinh, the best among the *Vaishnava*, has given pride of place to non-violence. This means that a man who has no love in him is no *Vaishnava*. One who does not follow truth and has not acquired control over all his senses is not a *Vaishnava*. He teaches us in his *prabhatiyan* that one does not become a *Vaishnava simply* by studying the Vedas, by following the rules of *varnashrama*, by wearing a string of basil seeds or the *tilak* mark. All these things can be the origin of sin. Even a hypocrite may wear a string of beads or put the *tilak* mark or study the Vedas or keep repeating Rama's name with his lips. But such a one cannot follow truth in his life, cannot, without giving up his hypocrisy, help people in distress or be self-controlled in speech, action and thought.

I invite everyone's attention to these principles, since I still continue to receive letters regarding Antyajas. The advice I receive from one and all is that, if I do not exclude Antyajas from the national schools, the movement for *swaraj* will end in smoke. If I have even a little of the true *Vaishnava* in me, God will also vouchsafe me the strength to reject the *swaraj* which may be won by abandoning the Antyajas.

The resolution, to the effect that the Antyajas cannot be excluded from any place which is open to members of other classes or communities, is not mine but that of the senate as a whole. I welcome the resolution. Had the senate not passed it, it would have been guilty of *adharma*.

The resolution lays down nothing new. One to the same effect is actually in operation in the existing schools. The Congress, a body which the *Vaishnavas* respect, has also passed such a resolution. They have not opposed it. I realize, however, that they honour me by criticizing me for having a hand in a resolution of this kind. The point of their argument is that others may violate *dharma* but that I, especially, should not do so. This is very gratifying to me.

I have been endeavouring to show that *dharma* requires that we do not look upon Antyajas as untouchables. Old veils prevent us from seeing that we are guilty of *adharma* in acting to the contrary. Just as, through such veils, British rule cannot see its own Satanism, so also, thanks to them, some of us are unable to see the chains of slavery which bind us. I think it my duty to reason with such people patiently.

But I cannot stand hypocrisy and sophistry. I saw in Gujarati an account of a talk I had with Maharajshri, as also the comments on it. I have been very much pained by both. I seldom comment on views expressed in newspapers. In fact I scarcely read papers. But the Gujarati is a widely read paper and it claims to present *sanatan dharma* in its true nature. Hence I am pained whenever I find in it even the least element of unfairness. A friend has sent me a cutting giving the report of my talk with Maharajshri and the criticism on it. I see in both an attempt, deliberate or otherwise, to prove *adharma* to be *dharma*. I shall explain next time what this is.

Many among you are my relations, many belong to the same community as I do and many of you are my friends from childhood days. From all these I get letters. In some of them the correspondents compliment me on my views about Antyajas, in some others they gently remonstrate with me, thinking that I am in error in holding these views, in some the correspondents treat me to harsh words in their anger and in some they actually hold out threats against me.

I regard all these things as a sign of their love for me. There are many others, besides me, who hold the same views about Antyajas as I do and do not object to contact with them, but people are angry with me and the reason, as I understand it, is that they believe that, in all other respects, I follow the restraints of *dharma* to the utmost and am otherwise a good man. They cannot reconcile themselves to what they believe to be my erroneous views about Antyajas. They think that these views hold up our progress towards *swaraj*. Some even believe that I have gone out of my way to invite trouble and have, in my obstinacy, endangered the ship of *swaraj*.

My own humble belief, against this, is that my concern for Antyajas is a credit to my devotion to the *Vaishnava* way of life, that it is an expression of pure compassion, and that it proves my scrupulous regard for the restraints of religious life.

Some *Vaishnavas* believe that I am destroying *varnashrama*. On the contrary, I believe that I am trying to cleanse it of impurities and so reveal its true form. I am certainly not advocating abolition of restrictions on eating and drinking in company with anyone and everyone or on intermarrying among communities. I merely say that the idea that physical contact with some person is a sin is itself sinful.

The attempt to defend the practice of untouchability by citing the similar practice of avoiding contact with a woman during the period of menstruation does not convince me. A chance contact with a woman during this time is not looked upon as a sin. It is held to be violation of a rule of hygiene and so the person takes a bath to be clean again. If anyone avoided contact with an Antyaja who had been engaged in sanitary work and had not bathed or otherwise cleansed himself after the work, or in case he had contact with such an Antyaja, went and had a bath, I can understand the idea. But my conscience can never accept the idea that *dharma* requires us to keep away scrupulously from everyone born an Antyaja.

The inspiration of the *Vaishnava* way is compassion. I do not see a trace of this in our treatment of the Antyajas. Many among us never address an Antyaja except with a word of contempt. If an Antyaja is ever found sitting in the same compartment with other Hindus there win be a rain of abuse on him. We offer them food left over on our plates, as we do to cattle. If an Antyaja has fever or is bitten by a serpent, our *vaids* and doctors will refuse to go to his place and treat him. If anyone should get ready to go, we would do everything in our power to stop him. For their residence, the Antyajas get the worst localities, with no amenities like light and public streets. They are provided with no wells for their use. They cannot use public wells and *dharmsalas and* cannot attend schools. We expect from them the most difficult of services and pay them the least. The sky above and the earth below is all that they have by way of shelter. Is such treatment in keeping with the *vaishnava* way of life? Is it the way inspired by compassion; is it not rather the way of cruelty? The British Government, against which you have launched non-cooperation, does not treat us with such contempt. We actually cherish our Dyerism towards Antyajas as *dharma*.

Speaking for myself, I believe that we are reaping as we sowed. Treating the Antyajas with contempt, we have become objects of the entire world's contempt.

The idea of untouchability is unacceptable to reason. It is contrary to truth and non-violence and, therefore, is certainly not *dharma*. The very idea of our being high and others low is base. He is no true Brahmin who lacks the quality of the Sudra: readiness for service. He alone is a Brahmin who possesses the qualities of all others, the Kshatriya, the Vaisya and the Sudra and, in addition, has knowledge. A Sudra is not altogether devoid of knowledge. Readiness for service is predominant in him over his other qualities. The *varnashrama-dharma* has no room for distinctions of high and low. The *Vaishnava* tradition knows of *Bhangs* and *Chandals* who attained deliverance. How can a *dharma* which holds that the entire universe is permeated by Vishnu believe that He is not present in the Antyaja?

I have no desire, however, to interpret the *Shastras* to you. I do not claim to be a man of learning. Every *shastri* is welcome to have the better of me in interpreting the *Shastras*. I know with confidence that I have had some experience of what the way of compassion means. This way can have simply no room in it for an attitude of contempt for Antyajas.

Moreover, what people will you describe as Antyajas? Is a weaver an Antyaja? Are wealthy dealers in leather Antyajas? Or is it that gold cleanses everything? A *Chamarwho* has given up his traditional work, a *Bhangi* who has taken to driving a car or works in a mill, who takes a bath everyday and keeps himself clean, is even such a person an untouchable?

Why argue, however? So long as you believe that physical contact with anyone whom you regard as an untouchable is a sin, you may, if, you wish, take a bath after such contact, but my request to you is that just as you do not hold in disregard a mother who is in her period of menstruation, but serve her instead, so should you serve Antyajas instead of despising them. Dig wells for them, build schools for them, and arrange for *vaids* to visit them, make their suffering your own and so earn their heartfelt blessings. See to it that they have their homes in good areas. Pay them well, respect them, educate them, look upon them as your younger brothers and persuade them to give up drinking, beef-eating, etc. Reward those who do these things. If you act in this way, you will come to see that the idea of untouchability is (as the poet says) a superfluous limb. Some of you have refused to contribute to the Tilak Swaraj Fund simply because of my views regarding Antyajas. This is my appeal to you, however, contribute money for the reform of untouchables. You can certainly do so, even if you do not abandon the practice of untouchability. Actually, some *Vaishnavas* have earmarked their contributions for this purpose. Moreover, though you may not like my views about Antyajas, you can surely give some money for the *swadeshi* movement, for famine-relief and for schools. I believe, though that you would certainly not oppose improvement in the conditions of Antyajas, and, therefore, appeal to you that, as evidence of such regard for the principle of compassion, you earmark your contributions for activities intended for their uplift.

CHAPTER-19

A Sadhu in Ochre Robes

We publish here a dialogue exactly as it took place only a few days ago. To make it interesting to the readers, some of the sentences have been broken up and the picture of Hind Devi has been touched up a little. Except for these changes, the questions and answers are reproduced exactly as they occurred. The value of the dialogue lies in the fact that it actually took place. The names of the speakers have been purposely left out:

A : Jai Sachchidananda. I wonder if you recognize me?

B : You did not have this ochre robe on then!

A : True, father, I was initiated into this dress by a certain *mahatma*.

B : Did you not give any thought to the matter?

A : I had faith in the *mahatma*. I used to reflect a little on religion, and so I know that what the *mahatma* advised could be done.

B : Do people revere you when they see you in this dress?

A : Yes, father, they do, to be sure.

B : Are you worthy of such reverence?

A : Oh, no. How can I claim that I am? I am full of attachments and aversions.

B : You beg for alms, no doubt?

A : Yes. I do.

B : Do you say anything when receiving the alms?

A : Not much, but occasionally I do preach.

B : Have you done any study?

A : Only a little. I have read a few *shastras* in Prakrit.

B : Are you happy leading such a life?

A : I wish I were! This is an idle quest in which I am engaged. I would certainly do what is good for me. Can you show me the way?

B : I should very much like to ask you to discard this dress, and that is easily done. But now it is better to think how best you may live so as to be worthy of it.

A : Indeed, that would be best.

B : I know well enough that you are a devotee of Hind Devi.

A : I have not thought about the matter.

B : I fancy that the Goddess wears a *sari* made in Japan. The sleeves of her satin blouse made in Paris are bordered with Parisian lace. On her forehead is a small vermilion mark made with imported stuff. On her wrists are English bangles. In her right hand are spikes of *bajri*, glittering like gold and of *jowar with* grains like pearls. In her left hand is a bit of rotten, dusty cotton thread. The Devi has the colour of the wheat near by; her face is downcast; she looks as if she had been crying. Around her, her children, evidently famished, are with painful slowness working in the fields. On the left are spinning-wheels covered with white ants; the cotton-strings round the wheels have snapped, the spindle-holders are about to drop down; around her tire seated our womenfolk, dozing. A few weavers are engaged in weaving bits of cloth.

A : Yes, that is a faithful picture of the Goddess.

B : Do you understand, then, what the Goddess is saying to both you and me?

A : To be sure, that we must work.

B : Yes, of course, it is that. He who performs no yajna, does no physical work, is a thief. That is what the 'Gita' says. But don't you think the Goddess is telling us something more than that?

A : Oh, do tell me, yourself.

B : From her looks, the Goddess seems to appeal to us that we should help her to be rid of those foreign garments, to clean the spinning- wheels for those sleepy women and set them spinning again.

A : What you say sounds as true as gold.

B : Well, then, we shall succeed in determining what you should do, so that you may live as befits your ochre robe. Many a *sadhu* dishonours his robe. These are a burden on the nation; you will surely admit as much!

A : No one can deny it.

B : Then, you should learn spinning and weaving, teach them to others and so ensure their and your regeneration. Your spinning-wheel will preach for you.

A : Indeed, I feel I have been rather hasty in donning this robe. My intention was good, but now I shall lose no time to pick up spinning and weaving.

Notes: